Great Birding Spots

in
Wakulla, Leon & Franklin Counties
Florida

Editor: Larry Thompson

Writers: Julie Duggan & Jack Dozier

Copy Editor: Anne C. Petty

Cover Photos: Charles Lee

Financial Sponsors: Carlton & Rebecca Duggan

Gene & Mary Louise Ellis

Tallahassee Nurseries

Andrew Jubal Smith

Apalachee Audubon Society, Inc., Tallahassee

© 2003 by Apalachee Audubon Society, Inc. All rights reserved.
Printed in the United States of America

ISBN 0-9724873-0-1

Maps & Cover Design by Lyons Digital Media
        Jonathan Lyons, Principal Designer
        Julie Walker, Production Artist

Printing by Graphic Press

Front Cover: Great Egret in breeding plumage

The Apalachee Audubon Society wishes to thank Mrs. Henry M. Stevenson for permission to use information from her late husband's *Field Card of Florida Birds*.

The Society also expresses its appreciation to the following individuals for generously sharing their time, talents, and knowledge in the preparation of this book:

Bonnie Jean Allen, Bald Point State Park

Randy Bond, Southeast Farm Wastewater Reuse Facility

Julie Brashears, Florida Fish and Wildlife Conservation Commission

Barry Burch, St.. George Island State Park

Jim Cox, Tall Timbers Research Station

Darby Dressel, Thomas P. Smith Water Reclamation Facility

Dr. Frances James, Florida State University

Mike Keyes, St. Marks National Wildlife Refuge

Clair Laba-Ragans

Thom Lewis, St. Vincent National Wildlife Refuge

Eric Lovestrand, Apalachicola National Estuarine Research Reserve

Barbara Lyons

Kate Malone

Gil Nelson

Perry Odom, City of Tallahassee

Roy Ogles, Apalachicola National Estuarine Research Reserve

Harry Qualls

Joe Reinman, St. Marks National Wildlife Refuge

Scott Savery, Wakulla Springs State Park

Ellen & Jim Shelton

Rick West

MarkWielgorecki, Ochlockonee River State Park

Robin Will, St. Marks National Wildlife Refuge

Contents

About
Wakulla, Leon & Franklin Counties

The Wakulla/Leon/Franklin-County area lies in the eastern Panhandle of Florida from the Georgia state line to the Gulf of Mexico. Beyond the borders of its principal city—Tallahassee—the extensive human development found in other parts of Florida has been slow in coming, so much of the natural habitat still exists. Development is relatively light even in the coastal areas, although this is likely to change as time goes by.

One factor in favor of habitat preservation is the amount of public land in this area. Much of the 564,000-acre Apalachicola National Forest—the largest national forest in Florida—lies in Wakulla, Leon, and Franklin counties. A good portion of Wakulla County's coastal lands and a 12,226-acre island in Franklin County are set aside as national wildlife refuges. In addition to these federal holdings, pockets of land owned by the State of Florida and The Nature Conservancy are protected from uses causing adverse effects on wildlife.

The area covered by this book spans two distinctly different physiographic regions separated by an east-west topographic break known as the Cody Escarpment. North of the scarp lies the Tallahassee Red Hills region, characterized by gently rolling hills of red-clay soils, pine forests, and hardwood hammocks. Elevations along the scarp drop 15 to 20 feet to the Gulf Coast Lowlands. You can see the scarp just south of the Florida State Capitol in Tallahassee, looking south from the North Florida Fairgrounds on South Monroe Street.

The overstory of the pine forests in the Tallahassee Red Hills region consists mostly of longleaf pine, while the understory supports several species of oak, including turkey oak. The ground cover includes an assortment of forbs and grasses but is dominated by wiregrass. The hammocks of the Tallahassee Red Hills are primarily deciduous southern mixed-hardwood forests of American beech, white oak, spruce pine, southern magnolia, and approximately 30 other, mostly deciduous, trees.

Below the Cody Escarpment, the land flattens out into the sandy Gulf Coast Lowlands terminating in a fringe of sandy dunes in the western portions and, in the east, in broad expanses of black needlerush-dominated saltmarsh grading gently into the Gulf. The coastal lowlands are characterized by pine flatwoods and depression swamps. The overstory includes longleaf pine in the drier areas, slash pine in the mesic areas, and pond pine in wetter sites. The shrub layer is often dominated by saw palmetto intermixed with a large assortment of wildflowers. The depression swamps, known locally as bay swamps or bays, contain

1

standing water much of the year and support a lush vegetation of sweetbay magnolia, swamp bay, loblolly bay, black gum, and water tupelo as well as fetterbush and staggerbush.

Tallahassee, the area's only city, is Florida's state capital and home to Florida A&M University, Florida State University and Tallahassee Community College. Although the city retains the character of a relaxed college town, it has not escaped the development affecting all Florida cities, and its boundaries continue to sprawl into the surrounding countryside. Tallahassee has been called "a city in a forest," a description still largely accurate despite the ever-widening fields of asphalt.

Unspoiled nature and a relatively low degree of development prevail as you travel south of Tallahassee into Wakulla County. Much of the county's coastal area is dedicated to St. Marks National Wildlife Refuge, arguably Florida's best Refuge in terms of bird diversity and the ease with which birds can be seen. Inland, the headwaters of the lovely Wakulla River emerge at Wakulla Spring, one of the largest and deepest freshwater springs in the world.

The historic town of Apalachicola lies 80 miles southwest of Tallahassee at the mouth of the Apalachicola River. During the nineteenth century, "Apalach" was a thriving cotton port and today is undergoing a renaissance as historical houses and commercial buildings are restored by local property owners and businesspeople. The clean waters of adjacent Apalachicola Bay produce more than 90 percent of Florida's oysters, 10 percent of the national supply.

Hotel accommodations can be found in Tallahassee, Panacea, Apalachicola, at Wakulla Springs State Park, and on St. George Island. On fall "football weekends"—when one of the university teams is playing at home—beds can be scarce in Tallahassee, so be sure to call ahead. The Apalachicola National Forest and most state parks mentioned in this book have public campgrounds.

The importance of birders to Florida's economy is recognized by the State through its support of the Great Florida Birding Trail. The 2000-mile highway trail links birding sites throughout the state and is expected to be completed in 2006.

When Is the Best Season for Birding?

The pleasantly cool temperatures of fall, winter, and spring coincide with the most interesting birding times in the eastern Panhandle. Summer offers good birding too, but it takes a sturdy constitution to brave the muggy heat, which can be intense even in early morning.

Fall migration begins as early as late July and reaches its peak in October. In fall, savvy birders watch the weather forecasts for cold fronts that push high concentrations of migrants out of the skies and into vegetation. The hours just before a cold front arrives and about two days after it passes are the best times for migrant fallouts. Fall is also a good time to observe hawks as they congregate at the coast, awaiting the right weather conditions for a Gulf crossing.

Spring migrations begin in late February and continue through April. Of shorter duration than fall migrations, they are most spectacular along the Gulf Coast. Fewer migrants are seen inland, perhaps because birds returning in spring tend to descend at first sight of land and recuperate for a while on the coast before continuing to their next stop in the woods and fields in Georgia.

In winter, the coastal areas, inland fields, and forests attract an interesting array of wintering birds, including the occasional rarity.

Climate & Conditions

Temperatures averages for Tallahassee and Apalachicola are shown in the table on page 4. The average humidity in Tallahassee ranges from 90 percent at dawn to 55 percent in the late afternoon; the humidity range in Apalachicola is 87 percent to 65 percent. Monthly precipitation ranges from 4 to 9 inches; summer months see the most rain, usually in the form of afternoon thundershowers.

Biting insects are usually not a problem in cooler weather, but during warm periods they can spoil a birding excursion. Insect repellent will fend off most pests. During warm weather, watch in open areas for the raised dirt mounds marking the underground colonies of fire ants, which can inflict painful bites.

The Florida Panhandle is home to four species of poisonous snakes, but it takes real effort to find one and none will bite unless they feel trapped or otherwise threatened. When tramping through vegetation, exercise normal care, and if you see a snake, stay out of its way.

Average Daily Temperatures

Month	Tallahassee High/Low	Apalachicola High/Low
January	64°/40° F	61°/44° F
February	67°/41° F	63°/46° F
March	73°/48° F	69°/53° F
April	80°/53° F	76°/60° F
May	86°/62° F	82°/66° F
June	90°/69° F	87°/72° F
July	91°/71° F	89°/74° F
August	91°/72° F	88°/74° F
September	88°/68° F	86°/71° F
October	81°/57° F	79°/61° F
November	72°/47° F	71°/53° F
December	66°/41° F	64°/47° F

Source: Sperling's Best Places Climate Statistics

The sites described in this book are all on public land or on private land open to the public during specific hours. When birding, please stay in designated areas and do not trespass on adjacent private property. Be courteous to others using birding sites for other purposes; they can often offer information about recent bird sightings.

St. George Island & Apalachicola Area

Franklin County's most notable birding locations lie in this coastal area on the Gulf of Mexico:

1 St. George Island State Park (page 6)

2 Unit 4 of Apalachicola National Estuarine Research Reserve (page 9)

3 Nature Walk at Apalachicola National Estuarine Research Reserve Nature Center (page 10)

4 Apalachicola Bird Island (page 13)

5 St. Vincent National Wildlife Refuge (page 14)

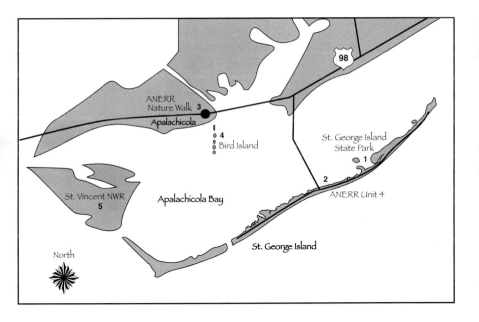

1   St. George Island State Park

The largest of Franklin's County's four barrier islands, St. George is the only one linked to the mainland by bridge. In the mid-1960's, just before completion of the bridge paved the way for private development, the eastern third of the island was wisely reserved as a state park.

During migrations and in winter, birding can be good throughout the island, but in spring, your first stop should be the park's Youth Camp, an open woodland on the bay side that consistently attracts a variety of resting migrants. In the wake of a cold front, the possibilities can be truly amazing. (From the entrance station, proceed 0.7 mi., turn left, and park in the lot near the restrooms.) Commonly seen in the open woods of the camp—especially around the restrooms—are **Yellow-billed Cuckoo**, **Red-eyed Vireo**, **House Wren**, **Veery**, **Gray Catbird**, **Cape May Warbler**, **Blackpoll Warbler**, **Black-and-white Warbler**, **American Redstart**, **Prothonotary Warbler**, **Hooded Warbler**, **Scarlet Tanager**, **Rose-breasted Grosbeak**, **Indigo Bunting**, **Painted Bunting**, **Bobolink**, and **Orchard Oriole**.

From Apalachicola:

Take US 98 east over the bridge and turn right (south) on FL 300. Cross the bridge to St. George Island and turn left (east) on Gulf Beach Dr. Proceed 4 mi. to park entrance.

From Apalachicola National Estuarine Research Reserve Unit 4:

From the Reserve entrance, turn left (east) on East Pine Ave. and continue about 2.2 mi. until the road connects to Gulf Beach Dr. Turn left and proceed about 2 mi. to the park entrance.

The boat ramp at the end of the Youth Camp road offers a good view of the bayshore and waters where you are likely to observe wintering sea ducks and year-round wading birds such as the nesting **American Oystercatcher** and **Willet**.

Along the park's main road, check the power lines for **American Kestrel**, migrating kingbirds (**Western**, **Eastern**, and **Gray**) and **Scissor-tailed Flycatcher**. **Ospreys**, which nest on the island, and **Bald Eagles** frequently soar overhead. In September/October, the park is an excellent place to observe the hawk migrations, most notably the departures of **Northern Harrier**, **Sharp-shinned Hawk**, **Cooper's Hawk**, **Merlin**, and **Peregrine Falcon**. Look for these raptors feeding as they fly over the sand dunes near the road or resting on the power lines.

From the Youth Camp road, turn left and go 3.6 mi. to a left turn leading to the park's campground—another promising location for migrants. Cruise slowly through the campground, looking for migrating grosbeaks, buntings, and **Shiny Cowbird**s attracted to the bird feeders occasionally provided by campers. During migration, check the brushy areas along the road here and elsewhere for **White-crowned Sparrow** and **Painted**

Bunting. **Gray Kingbird**s nest around the campground in summer and can be seen from spring through fall.

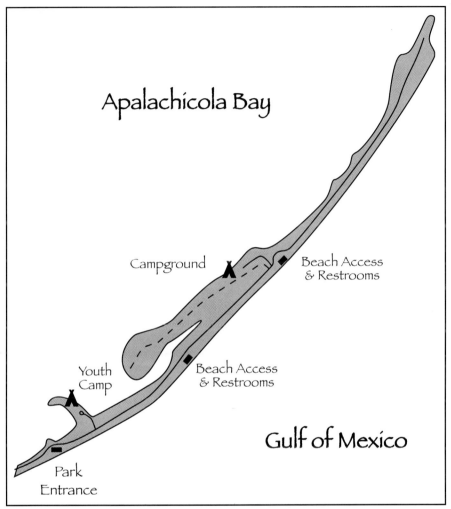

Apalachicola Bay

Campground

Beach Access & Restrooms

Youth Camp

Beach Access & Restrooms

Gulf of Mexico

Park Entrance

St. George Island State Park

A short way down the main road east of the campground is the second of two large parking areas for beachgoers. Park here and walk northeast up the beach. As you get away from the crowds, you'll find wading birds, shorebirds, and gulls. **Snowy Plover**s nest in the dry sand of the dunes near the point where the paved road ends and **Wilson's Plover** can be found on the beach here or on the bay side of the island. In winter, scan the waters for **Northern Gannet**, **Common Goldeneye**, scoters, and other sea ducks.

During migrations, western accidentals such as **Lesser Nighthawk, Rock Wren, Yellow-headed Blackbird, Curve-billed Thrasher,** and **Western Tanager** have been observed on St. George Island.

Most of the eastern end of St. George Island has been proposed by the U.S. Fish and Wildlife Service as Critical Habitat for **Piping Plovers.**

St. George Island State Park

Restrooms	Yes
Off-Highway Parking	Yes
Birding from Car	Yes
Terrain	Easy
Entrance Fee	Standard state park fee
Limited Hours/Days	8 a.m. to sunset daily
Permission to Enter	Not required
Note	To enter the park earlier than 8 a.m., stop by the entrance station prior to your early-morning visit and purchase a recreation pass, which will include the combination to the front gate's lock. A week's pass is $13.25.

2 Unit 4 of Apalachicola National Estuarine Research Reserve

This small, newly established site offers a nice adjunct to birding at St. George Island State Park. It's a wooded area with quick access to the bayshore. In spring, Unit 4 is worth checking for neotropical migrants—vireos, warblers, tanagers, buntings, and orioles. In fall, it's a good spot to observe raptor migrations.

Next to the gazebo, a metal gate marks the trail head for three short paths, to the east, west, and straight ahead to the bay.

The right-hand trail takes you about 75 yards east through the open woods, a promising area for spring migrants and woodpeckers. The trail passes several small ponds before petering out in the brush. Here it's wise to turn around; bushwhacking beyond the end of the trail may disturb a Cottonmouth.

From Apalachicola:

Take US 98 east over the bridge and turn right (south) on FL 300. Cross the bridge to St. George Island and turn left (east) on E. Pine Ave. Proceed 0.8 mi. to Sixth St. East and turn left. Sixth St. ends at the site entrance. Park next to the gazebo.

From St. George Island State Park:

Take Gulf Beach Dr. west approx 3.5 miles to Sixth St. East and turn right. Sixth St. ends at the site entrance. Park next to the gazebo.

The center trail leads straight to the beach and shallow waters on the edge of Apalachee Bay, and the left-hand trail accesses the beach, more woodland ponds, and tidal pools. Wading birds, shorebirds, and ducks are all good possibilities here.

Unit 4 of Apalachicola National Estuarine Research Reserve

Restrooms	No
Off-Highway Parking	Yes
Birding from Car	No
Terrain	Easy
Entrance Fee	No
Limited Hours/Days	8 a.m. to sunset
Permission to Enter	Not required

3 Nature Walk at Apalachicola National Estuarine Research Reserve

The Reserve's 246,000 acres encompass Apalachicola Bay, a good chunk of the adjacent barrier islands and mainland, and the lower 52 miles of the Apalachicola River floodplain. An extensive description of this important natural system is not possible here, but if the Nature Center is open when you visit, take a moment to pick up the brochure on their mission and activities. The Center also has a bird list, but it covers the entire Reserve area, not just the Nature Walk.

Take US 98 to Apalachicola. At the intersection where US 98 turns west, go north on Market St. When the road ends at the marina (0.7 mi. from the US 98 turnoff), turn left and proceed a short distance to the Nature Center entrance. Park immediately inside the entrance. The Nature Walk trail head is across the parking lot from the Nature Center.

The Nature Walk has been open only three years and is just becoming an established site among area birders. The quarter-mile trail is, for the most part, a raised wooden boardwalk meandering through astonishingly lovely swamp terrain. Even if no birds were present, the walk would be worthwhile as it affords opportunities for close observation of swamp plants. For wildflower enthusiasts, spring is a good time to catch blooming Blue Flag Iris, spiderwort, and magnolia.

In the parking lot, as you apply the insect repellent advisable for unharrassed enjoyment of this site, check the trees overhead for **Cedar Waxwing** (fall through spring), **Barn Swallow**, and **Common Grackle**. Then proceed down the walk, through the tunnel formed by the dense underbrush, listening for **Northern Parula** (spring) and **Hermit Thrush** (fall through early spring). Common migrants in spring and fall are **Ruby-throated Hummingbird**, **Red-eyed Vireo**, **Gray Catbird**, **Cape May Warbler**, **American Redstart**, **Northern Waterthrush**, **Summer Tanager**, **Scarlet Tanager**, and **Blue Grosbeak**.

A short distance from the trail head, the trail crosses an old asphalt path. From this point on, check the cabbage palms and other low tree branches for **Barred Owl**. This species has been reported roosting quite close to the trail, allowing birders an inspection without the need for binoculars.

As you enter the swamp, the scallop-shell path gives way to a raised wooden boardwalk crossing first through a cabbage-palm hammock and then through a thicket of willows offering cover for smaller birds. Here look for **Ruby-crowned Kinglet** (fall through winter), **Common Yellowthroat**, **Blue-gray Gnatcatcher** (fall through spring), **Yellow-throated Warbler** (fall through spring), **Swamp Sparrow**, and **White-**

throated Sparrow (fall)—all are easiest to see in winter and in early spring before the vegetation thickens. **Indigo Bunting** is a regular here in spring and has been observed during fall migrations as well. As you pass through the swamp, look for secretive wading birds such as **Green Heron** and **Black-crowned** and **Yellow-crowned Night-Heron**.

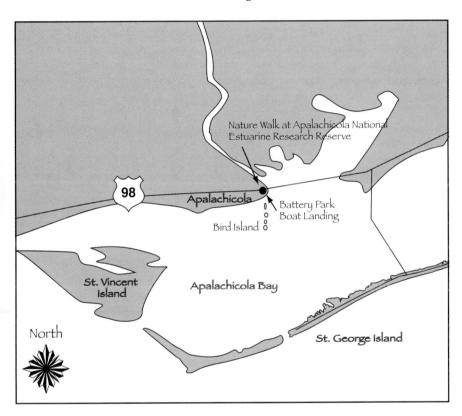

When the boardwalk enters a hardwood hammock, listen for the raucous **Boat-tailed Grackle** and **Yellow-billed Cuckoo**. **Downy Woodpecker**, **Northern Flicker**, and **Red-bellied Woodpecker** are year-round residents here, and **Yellow-bellied Sapsucker** appears from fall through spring. This portion of the trail is also good for **Brown-headed Nuthatch**. Although most of these birds are year-round residents, they are more likely to be seen along the trail in late fall.

The boardwalk emerges from the swamp to cross an open area encircled by Southern Red Cedar bushes. This area was a spoil site created by dredging for the nearby marina. The break in the tree canopy offers a good opportunity to scan the sky for **Chimney Swift** and **Bald Eagle**. After a short distance, the boardwalk reenters the swamp and begins a slow ascent through the trees before it emerges into the open marsh and terminates in a high observation deck.

The deck commands a broad view of the saltmarsh and Scipio Creek, a narrow offshoot of the Apalachicola River. About 500 yards to the northwest lies Turtle Harbor, a shallow, 10-acre pond that attracts waterfowl but requires a scope for adequate viewing from the deck. The waters of Turtle Harbor and Scipio Creek are good for **Pied-billed Grebe, Double-crested Cormorant, Wood Duck, Gadwall, American Wigeon, Blue-winged Teal, Lesser Scaup, Common Moorhen,** and **American Coot.** Turtle Harbor often attracts small numbers of other diving and dabbling ducks, so look carefully for less common species such as **Mallard, Northern Pintail, Green-winged Teal,** and **Ring-necked Ducks.** Scipio Creek is a favored fishing spot for herons, egrets, terns, **Belted Kingfisher,** and **Osprey.** The tall marsh grasses are nesting grounds for **Clapper Rail;** approach the observation deck quietly and you may hear their call or even see one skulking among the grass. **Black Rail** has also been heard, but rarely. In spring, flocks of migrant **Bobolinks** congregate in the marsh, and in winter **Nelson's Sharp-tailed Sparrow** may flush from the grass.

The skies above the marsh are good for **American White Pelican** (fall and spring), **Swallow-tailed** and **Mississippi Kites** (summer), **Purple Martin, Tree Swallow,** and **Northern Harrier** (winter). Scan the treeline for perching **Bald Eagle** (fall through spring), **Red-tailed Hawk,** and other raptors. If you happen to see a crow, listen for the nasal "caw" that distinguishes the **Fish Crow** from the more vocally powerful American Crow. Fly-overs from Bird Island, a multi-species nesting area in the nearby bay, might include **Brown Pelican, Caspian** and **Royal Terns,** and other coastal birds.

Nature Walk at Apalachicola National Estuarine Research Reserve

Restrooms	When Visitor Center is open: 8 a.m. to 5 p.m. weekdays
Off-Highway Parking	Yes
Birding from Car	No
Terrain	Easy
Entrance Fee	No
Limited Hours/Days	Daylight hours
Permission to Enter	Not required

4 Apalachicola Bird Island

Bird Island is a finger-shaped spoil area at the mouth of the Apalachicola River. Created in 1995 as an alternative breeding area for **Least Terns** and **Black Skimmers**, the island has become an important nesting and wintering ground for large numbers of pelicans, shorebirds, gulls, and terns. The Least Terns, whose nesting areas on the St. George Island causeway were being disturbed by traffic, nested for a while on Bird Island, but eventually moved on to other locations.

By boat from Apalachicola:

Launch at the Battery Park boat landing just below the John Gorrie Bridge. Proceed in a south/southeasterly direction for about a half mile, exercising care when crossing the mouth of the river.

From the Apalachicola causeway:

From Apalachicola, cross the John Gorrie Bridge and pull off the highway on the right when you reach the causeway.

The island lies about a half mile out in the bay from Apalachicola, so it's best seen from a boat. Because the birds are sensitive to disturbance year-round, come no closer than 50 to 100 yards from the island. In good weather, the island is easily reached by canoe or kayak if you launch at low tide and then use the incoming tide to assist in your return to the mainland. Timing the return trip around an incoming tide will also help you avoid strong currents at the mouth of the river. From April through August, the island is closed to protect the breeding colony, but you can still see plenty from the boat.

At low tide, some of the island's birds spread to the flats lying closer to the causeway and can be seen with a scope or binoculars.

Nesting birds in summer include **Brown Pelican** (more than 250 pairs were observed in 2001), **American Oystercatcher**, and **Gull-billed**, **Caspian**, **Sandwich**, and **Least Terns**.

In winter, the island is a roosting place for **Double-crested Cormorant**, **Brown Pelican**, gulls (including **Lesser Black-backed Gull**) and terns. Inhabiting the grasses around the edge of the island are winter sparrows such as **Field**, **Savannah**, **Nelson's Sharp-tailed**, **Song**, and **Swamp Sparrows**.

Apalachicola Bird Island

Restrooms	No
Off-Highway Parking	At boat ramp but not on causeway.
Birding from Car	No
Terrain	Easy
Entrance Fee	No
Limited Hours/Days	Daylight. Low tide is best.
Permission to Enter	Not required

5   St. Vincent National Wildlife Refuge

Most barrier islands are little more than skinny bands of sand, but St. Vincent is different. It has beaches, of course—nine miles of deserted shore bordered in some places by towering dunes. But over time, an unusual combination of wind and water currents has enabled St. Vincent to develop an uncharacteristic girth. Four miles wide at its broadest point, the island contains extensive uplands and interior wetlands not usually found on barrier islands. Its inland topography undulates from ridges clad in huge live oaks to low pine swales dotted with freshwater ponds.

> **From Apalachicola:**
>
> Go west on US 98, bear left on CR 30A, and turn left on CR 30B (Indian Pass Rd). The boat ramp is at the end of the road. Boat across Indian Pass (1/4 mi.) and dock at the island away from the beach side.

The Refuge encompasses the entire island—more than 12,000 acres. Uninhabited by humans and accessible only by boat, it is best reached by crossing Indian Pass from Indian Peninsula to the western end of the island. In good weather, the quarter-mile trip is easily made by canoe or kayak. Currents in Indian Pass are sometimes strong but are mildest at slack and incoming tides. Once across the pass, you can walk along the beach or follow the sand roads inland. Avoid the western tip of the island at Indian Pass because it is closed year-round for nesting/resting shorebirds. Refuge staff say that St. Vincent's reputation as a haven for larger-than-average populations of poisonous snakes is unfounded; nevertheless they recommend you stick to the roads when walking inland.

The best times to bird the island are the cooler months from fall through spring. Three deer hunts are held during this period, though, so contact the Refuge office before you go to verify the Refuge is open to birders. Summer excursions are advisable only for those unfazed by oppressively humid heat and aggressive biting insects. Take along plenty of water.

The wooded inlands are good year-round for **Red-bellied Woodpecker, Downy Woodpecker, Brown-headed Nuthatch, Carolina Wren, Pine Warbler,** and **Eastern Towhee.** The large wading birds (**Great Blue Heron, Great Egret, Snowy Egret, Little Blue Heron, Tricolored Heron, White Ibis,** and **Wood Stork**) are common in and around the ponds, and a mixed-egret rookery is near Lake 5. This area is closed from October 1 through May 15, but the willows around Lake 5 are used as a roost year-round. Seven **Bald Eagle** nesting territories were counted in 2001.

In winter, check the beach for wading birds and shorebirds such as **Black Skimmer;** scan offshore for ducks and scoters. If you explore inland, keep in mind that the area around the impoundments on the southeastern corner of the island is closed in winter to prevent interference with nesting Bald Eagles and wintering waterfowl.

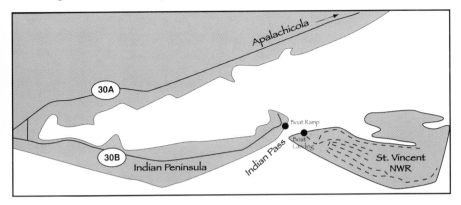

Access to St. Vincent National Wildlife Refuge

In the fall, large concentrations of raptors, including **Sharp-shinned Hawk**, **Cooper's Hawk**, **Broad-winged Hawk**, **Peregrine Falcon**, and **Merlin**, occasionally assemble on the beaches in preparation for their southward migrations.

In spring and fall, look for neotropical migrants in the oak hammocks along the inland ridges. These ridges are the remnants of St. Vincent's different shorelines over the past 5000 years. They begin quite close to Indian Pass, so it's not necessary to venture very far inland to find the hardwood habitat sought by incoming migrants.

The island hosts a small number of Sambar Deer, a southeast-Asian species similar to the elk found in the American West. These animals were introduced by previous owners who used the island as a hunting reserve. They do not appear to have a negative impact on the island and are harmless to humans. Perhaps more importantly, the Refuge is a breeding site for the endangered Red Wolf. Consider yourself lucky if you catch a glimpse of one of these shy predators.

St. Vincent National Wildlife Refuge

Restrooms	No
Off-Highway Parking	No. Accessible by boat only.
Birding from Car	No
Terrain	Moderate
Entrance Fee	No
Limited Hours/Days	Daylight hours
Permission to Enter	Not required, but call Refuge office (850-653-8808) for information on current conditions before making the trip. The island is closed three times a year for deer hunts and other times due to wildfires

Ochlockonee River & Bay Area

This region includes birding sites in Wakulla and Franklin counties lying near the Ochlockonee River and Bay:

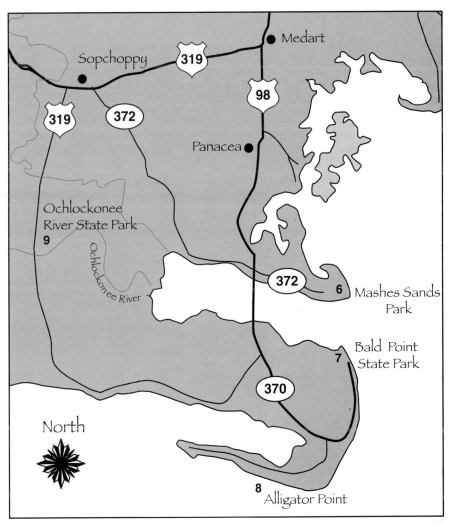

6   Mashes Sands County Park

The road to Mashes Sands takes you across a narrow salt marsh notable for its rail population. **Sora** is common here in winter, and the scarce **Yellow Rail** has been reported during migration. **Marsh Wrens**, present year-round, nest near the park entrance, and the environs also attract all the herons and egrets. At low tide, look for the occasional **Reddish Egret** feeding on the sandbars in the shallow waters off the beach.

> **From Panacea:**
>
> Go south on US 98 and turn left on CR 372 (Mashes Sands Rd.), which is just prior to the Ochlockonee Bay Bridge. Proceed 2.4 mi. to the park entrance. Park at the end of the road (2.6 mi.).

On maps, Mashes Sands looks like a hand with its forefinger crooked. The road runs along the arm and dead-ends at the wrist in a sandy parking area that can be crowded in summer, as Mashes Sands is a popular bathing beach with Wakulla Countians. You can walk down the beach in either direction.

In summer, **Gray Kingbirds** can easily be seen on power lines and in the trees as you approach the beach. When tides and human numbers are low, the beach swarms with gulls, terns, and shorebirds such as **Marbled Godwit**, **Whimbrel**, and flocks of **Black Skimmers**. From December to mid-Spring, a few **Bonaparte's Gulls** will be among them. At times these species can be seen resting on sandy points at both ends of the beach. **Horned Grebe** and **Bufflehead** are frequent offshore in winter, and occasionally **American Goldeneye** can be found around the oyster bars in the mouth of Ochlockonee Bay, south of the beach.

Mashes Sands County Park

Restrooms	Yes
Off-Highway Parking	Yes
Birding from Car	Yes
Terrain	Easy
Entrance Fee	Occasionally in summer, but nominal
Limited Hours/Days	No
Permission to Enter	Not required

7   Bald Point State Park

Bald Point State Park is a work in progress, one of Florida's newest parks in the process of being cobbled together through purchases of individual private landholdings. Overlooking Ochlockonee Bay, the park lies on the northern side of a long foot of land jutting into Apalachee Bay.

Bald Point's varied habitats—pine savannah, beach, and coastal shrub—attract avian variety, and its location makes it a magnet for trans-Gulf migrants. It is particularly noted in fall for **Cooper's**, **Sharp-shinned**, and other migrating hawks. More than 265 species have been reported on Bald Point, including such rarities as **Snowy Owl**.

Birding can be interesting all along Bald Point Dr., even before entering the park. In winter, check the roadside weeds and open pine understory for sparrows.

Approximately 1.7 mi. from the CR 370 intersection, check the freshwater ponds on the left for **King Rail**, **Virginia Rail**, and **Sora** (the latter two in winter). At 2.3 mi., where a small stream crosses the road, **Say's Phoebe**, **Western Kingbird**, and **Scissor-tailed Flycatcher** have been reported, primarily during fall migration, but sometimes in spring too.

From the Florida State Capitol building in Tallahassee (US 27 and FL 61):

Go south approximately 4.5 mi. on FL 61 (South Adams St.) to Capital Circle where US 319 joins. Continue south on US 319 (Crawfordville Hwy.) approximately 22 mi. to Medart. At the intersection where US 319 divides from US 98, continue going straight on US 98. From this intersection, go 10.0 mi., through Panacea and across the Ochlockonee Bay Bridge, and turn left on CR 370 (Alligator Dr.). Proceed 3.7 mi. to Bald Point Dr. and turn left. The park entrance is 2.8 mi. from the CR 370 intersection. Continue to the parking area at the end of the road (3.3 mi. from CR 370).

At 2.5 mi., park on the left (west) and take the half-mile-loop trail into the pinewoods where you are likely to see **Brown-headed Nuthatch**, **Eastern Bluebird**, and **Pine Warbler**. The trail winds past several small ponds where **Least Bitterns** have been observed nesting. The ponds are also reliable for rails.

The oak hammock area on the beach side (approximately 3.3 mi. from CR 370) is another reliable migrant trap. Park along the roadside and walk through the vegetation toward the beach to find migrating thrushes, catbirds (fall), and warblers. This area is good year-round for **Common Ground-Dove**, wrens, and **Eastern Towhee**.

The ponds on the left past the park entrance harbor **Virginia Rail** and **Sora**. Toward the end of the road in the marsh, **Clapper Rail** are abundant but difficult to see.

From the beach, look north toward the oyster bars in Ochlockonee Bay for **American Oystercatcher** and at the mouth of the bay for **Horned Grebe** and, in some winters, scoters. When present, scoters tend to congregate in a large raft just outside the mouth of the bay around the lighted buoy.

Bald Point State Park

Restrooms	Yes
Off-Highway Parking	Yes
Birding from Car	Yes
Terrain	Easy
Entrance Fee	No
Limited Hours/Days	8 a.m. to sunset
Permission to Enter	Not required on state-owned lands, but some areas in and around park may still be private. When in doubt, ask the park ranger before entering.

8   Alligator Point

Alligator Point has long been a quiet community of unassuming beach cottages overlooking the Gulf, owned mostly by families residing no farther away than Tallahassee. Although it's now being discovered by more far-flung city folk, Alligator Point still retains its simple charm. Public access to the beach is limited here, but if you are birding at Bald Point, it's worth the short drive to Alligator Point to check out the spots of birding interest on the southern side of the peninsula.

The roadside at the KOA campground (approximately 2.3 mi. from Bald Point Dr./6 mi. from US 98) is a good place to park and scan the waters for **Common Loon, Northern Gannet,** ducks, and scoters. Both **Red-throated** and **Pacific Loon** have been reported here, as has **White-winged Scoter.** Parking and beach access is also available further down Alligator Dr. at the public boat ramp (3.2 mi. from Bald Point Dr./7.2 mi. from US 98).

From the Florida State Capitol building in Tallahassee (US 27 and FL 61):

Go south approximately 4.5 mi. on FL 61 (South Adams St.) to Capital Circle where US 319 joins. Continue south on US 319 (Crawfordville Hwy.) approximately 22 mi. to Medart At the intersection where US 319 turns right, continue going straight on US 98. From this intersection, go 10.0 mi., through Panacea and across the Ochlockonee Bay Bridge and turn left on CR 370 (Alligator Dr.). Pass Bald Point Dr. (3.7 mi.) and bear right at the road fork.

In summer, look for **Gray Kingbirds** perching on power lines and in the beachside trees.

As you pass Alligator Harbor on the north side of the road, check the waters for **Horned Grebe, Bufflehead,** and **Red-breasted Merganser. Great Cormorant** has been recorded on the piers in the harbor and **American Avocet** is occasionally seen when tides are low.

The road dead-ends at the entrance to Phipps Preserve (4.8 mi. from Bald Point Dr./8.8 mi. from US 98), a Nature Conservancy property closed to public access. This end of Alligator Point is a migrant trap, offering the first landfall for trans-Gulf species arriving from South America. During spring migration, park at the gate and listen for birds.

Alligator Point

Restrooms	No
Off-Highway Parking	No
Birding from Car	Yes
Terrain	Easy
Entrance Fee	No
Limited Hours/Days	No
Permission to Enter	None required

9   Ochlockonee River State Park

Ochlockonee River State Park is perhaps best known for **Red-cockaded Woodpecker**, which nests in both bird-made and artificial tree cavities in the park. Two other sought-after species here are **Bachman's Sparrow**, which can be found year-round, and the wintering **Henslow's Sparrow**.

Within the park, a circular drive running through the open pinewoods offers promising birding opportunities. From the park office, continue 0.8 mi. through the parking area to a dirt road running past a picnic pavilion on your right. After entering the woods, look on the right for Red-cockaded Woodpecker cavities installed by biologists from St. Marks National Wildlife Refuge. All cavity trees in the park are denoted by white bands painted around the trunk about six feet up. The best times to find Red-cockaded Woodpeckers at their cavities are at dawn and dusk. During the day, the birds leave to forage for insects in the woods, but they usually remain within a mile's radius of their cavity, so it is possible to see them in the park throughout the day. The woods between the first group of cavities and the road fork (1.6 mi. from the park office) is a likely location for these woodpeckers. Cavity trees are also located at other sites along the loop road.

From the Florida State Capitol building in Tallahassee (US 27 and FL 61):

Go south approximately 4.5 mi. on FL 61 (South Adams St.) to Capital Circle where US 319 joins. Continue south on US 319 (Crawfordville Hwy.) approximately 22 mi. to Medart and turn right to continue on US 319 to Sopchoppy. From Sopchoppy, continue on US 319 for 4.0 mi. and turn left into the park entrance.

While driving through the pinewoods, also watch for **Eastern Wood-Pewee**, **Yellow-throated Vireo** (summer), **Brown-headed Nuthatch**, **Pine Warbler**, and **Bachman's Sparrow**. At the road fork, bear left and continue to the paved road where a right turn will return you to the park office.

In winter, check the park's wet, grassy areas for **Henslow's Sparrow**. **Chuck-will's-widow** and **Summer Tanager** are common throughout the park in summer, and **Barred Owl** can be found year-round in the hardwoods along the river.

Ochlockonee River State Park

Restrooms	Yes
Off-Highway Parking	Yes
Birding from Car	Yes
Terrain	Easy
Entrance Fee	Standard state park fee
Limited Hours/Days	8 a.m. until sunset
Permission to Enter	Not required

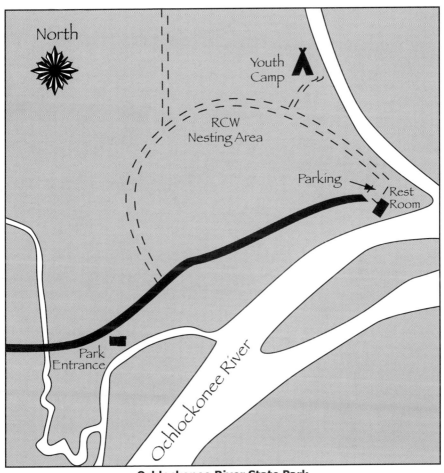

Ochlockonee River State Park

St. Marks National Wildlife Refuge & Wakulla Springs

St. Marks Refuge was established more than 70 years ago as a haven for wintering migratory birds. It comprises approximately 68,500 acres of forest, swamp, coastline, and salt marsh bordering Apalachee Bay in the Gulf of Mexico, plus another 30,000 acres of water in the bay where birds are protected.

The Refuge is divided into three units. The eastern unit—St. Marks—has facilities for human visitors and is well-known for its varieties of waterfowl, shorebirds, and migrants. Panacea and Wakulla—the western and central units, respectively—are less popular than their eastern sister, but nevertheless offer interesting birding possibilities.

More than 270 avian species are regularly seen throughout the year in the Refuge, and transient rarities are not unusual. In the winter of 2001-2002, a **Tropical Kingbird** made an extended stay, inciting a buzz of excitement throughout the birding community. For more than a decade now, the Refuge has been the wintering grounds for a small band of **Vermilion Flycatchers**. Ask at the Visitor Center whether they are present and where you can see them.

The Refuge Visitor Center at the top of Lighthouse Road is well worth an exploratory look—and it's a must if you have children in the party. The Center offers quite a good selection of naturalist books and exhibits of the animals who make their home in the Refuge. Free maps of the Refuge's hiking-trail system and a comprehensive bird list are available. Inside the front door you'll find a log of recent wildlife sightings.

Three birding sites are recommended in St. Marks Refuge:

10 Lighthouse Road (page 27)

11 Wakulla Beach Road (page 31)

12 Bottoms Road (page 33)

Wakulla Springs, a natural wonder a few miles north of the Refuge, attracts numerous avian species, both water and woodland, year-round:

13 Edward Ball Wakulla Springs State Park (page 35)

For non-birding activities, visit the Civil War-era Fort San Marcos de Apalachee State Park at the confluence of the St. Marks and Wakulla rivers. The nearby village of St. Marks was once the busy terminus of the railway from Tallahassee. Today the rail bed is a paved bike path drawing cyclists from the Tallahassee trail head to the fish eateries overlooking the river.

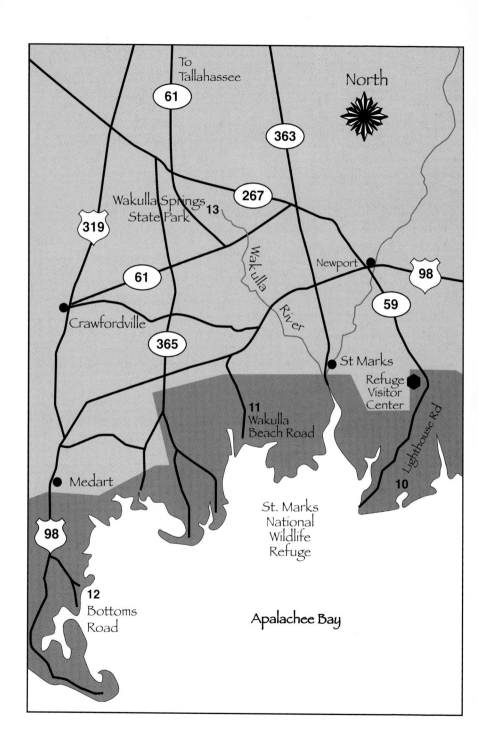

To
Tallahassee

61

North

363

267

Wakulla Springs
State Park **13**

319

Wakulla

Newport

98

61

River

59

Crawfordville

365

St Marks

Refuge
Visitor
Center

Lighthouse Rd

11
Wakulla
Beach Road

10

Medart

St. Marks
National
Wildlife
Refuge

98

12
Bottoms
Road

Apalachee Bay

10 Lighthouse Road

If your stay in the Wakulla-Leon-Franklin area allows time for only one excursion, make it Lighthouse Road in the Refuge. This paved route winds 6.5 mi. from a mixed hardwood/pine forest at the Refuge Visitor Center across a vast salt marsh dotted with large man-made pools to the historic St. Marks Lighthouse on Apalachee Bay.

Lighthouse Road is an excellent route for birders who prefer to ease along the road in a vehicle and set up scopes along the roadsides. For those who want to explore the Refuge away from the main road, it offers hiking trails along the ponds into wooded areas. In addition to birds, alligators are commonly found sunning along the poolsides, and it is not unusual to see wild boar in the forests. Black bear and bobcat reside in the Refuge but are rarely seen. In late October and early November, countless monarch butterflies pause at the Refuge before resuming their migration across the Gulf of Mexico.

From the Florida State Capitol building in Tallahassee (US 27 and FL 61):

Take FL 61 (South Monroe St.) south. On the south side of town, FL 363 joins FL 61. Stay on FL 363 (Woodville Hwy.) for approximately 10 mi. until you reach the blinking light at the intersection of FL 267. Turn left on FL 267. Proceed 3.7 mi. to US 98 and turn left. Go 0.5 mi. and turn right on CR 59 (Lighthouse Rd). Drive 3.5 mi. to the Refuge Visitor Center.

On the way to the Refuge Visitor Center, CR 59 passes through the Flintrock Wildlife Management Area, a privately owned hunting preserve that offers a couple of points of birding interest. In winter, **Henslow's Sparrows** may be observed along the power-line easement intersecting the road 0.9 mi. from US 98. Park on the roadside and walk west along the easement to flush out this species. In summer, check the young planted pines on both sides of the road for **Yellow-breasted Chat**, **Blue Grosbeak**, and **Indigo Bunting**. **Swallow-tailed Kite** and **Wild Turkey** have been seen along this road from about the Refuge gate (3.3 mi. from US 98) into the Refuge.

At the Refuge Visitor Center, check the wildlife log just inside the front door for birds and other creatures observed by recent visitors. If you are interested in hiking or just orienting yourself, maps are available inside along with an accurate bird list. In summer, step out on the back porch to scan Plum Orchard Pond for **Purple Gallinule**.

Before returning to your car, take a few minutes to stroll the Plum Orchard Pond Trail leading from the parking lot into the woods behind the Visitor Center. Skirting along the pond, the short (0.3 mi.) trail is a likely area in summer to observe nesting **Blue-gray Gnatcatcher** and warblers— **Northern Parula**, **Yellow-throated**, **Prothonotary**, and **Common Yellowthroat**. In winter, watch for roving flocks of wintering small birds (warblers, titmice, and chickadees) and look for **Golden-crowned Kinglet** in these mixed flocks.

To begin the Lighthouse Road tour, exit right from the Visitor Center parking lot and follow the road through the hardwood/pine/palm forest, keeping an eye out for **Wild Turkey**. At 0.8 mi.—a spot local birders call "Double Bridges"—making "pishing" sounds along the roadside can be productive during winter and migrations for **Northern** and **Louisiana Waterthrush**. Check the trees for **Acadian Flycatcher** and the brush along the creek for **Prothonotary Warbler**. This is another good spot for **Swallow-tailed Kite** overhead and in the woods, and for **Golden-crowned Kinglet** in mixed flocks.

Park at the Stoney Bayou/Deep Creek trail head (1.5 mi.) and explore the north end of Stoney Bayou Field, which runs south from the trail head for about a mile along the east side of Lighthouse Road. This grassy field— incidentally the Refuge's heliport—is excellent for **Sedge Wren** and wintering sparrows (most notably **Grasshopper** and **Henslow's**). In July and August, Stoney Bayou Field can be the site of amazing aerial exhibitions, when swarms of dragonflies attract numerous **Swallow-tailed** and **Mississippi Kites**, dipping and soaring in a feeding frenzy.

On the west side of Lighthouse Road (2.0 mi.), check the stand of dead pine snags for woodpeckers and nesting **Brown-headed Nuthatch**. Beyond the snags begin the pools—first East River Pool on the west, then on the east, a series of large impoundments separated by walkable dikes. The edges of East River Pool are reliable haunts for **Sora** and **Virginia Rail**. The once uncommon **Reddish Egret** is beginning to be seen more frequently here and **Least Bitterns** have been reported nesting around its edges.

All the pools are good year-round for herons and egrets, and in winter for ducks and other waterbirds. When water levels are favorable, the East River Pool and the Mounds Pools along the west side of the road are excellent for shorebirds. In addition to the usual inland shorebirds, such as **Greater** and **Lesser Yellowlegs** and **Stilt Sandpiper**, the pools are a good place in winter for **Long-billed Dowitcher**. Favorable water conditions in Mounds Pool also attract **Glossy Ibis** and **Black-necked Stilt**, which are seen from spring to late summer. **American Avocets** are unpredictable visitors to the Refuge, but when they are here, you will find them in the pools. **Bald Eagles** may be observed sitting in the tall trees on islands in the marshes beyond the pools.

At Headquarters Pond (5.0), park and take the quarter-mile trail to the observation platform, situated in view of a **Double-crested Cormorant** rookery. The platform is a good place to watch nesting herons, egrets, **White Ibis**, **Purple Gallinule**, and (in winter and early spring) nesting

Bald Eagle. Check the pond edges for **Virginia Rail** and **Sora** and the small grassy islands for nesting **Least Bittern**. **Black-crowned Night-Herons** appear at dawn and dusk on the low branches of trees edging the pond. In spring, the hardwood trees and shrubs surrounding the restrooms at Headquarters Pond is one of the best areas in the Refuge for migrant fallouts. Numerous species of transient woodland birds—cuckoos, vireos, thrushes, and warblers—have been reported here. In winter, try calling up **Whip-poor-wills**. You may also see **Eastern Screech-Owl**, **Great Horned Owl**, and **Barred Owl** in the vicinity.

A popular gathering spot for wintering ducks is Tower Pond, which is near Headquarters Pond beyond sight of the road. To see the pond, take the mile-long Mounds Interpretive Trail, which begins at the restroom building. As you walk along the trail, check the tall trees for the huge nests built by **Bald Eagles**. **Black Rail** nests throughout the Refuge and can be heard in May, but a reliable place to actually see this elusive species is in the marsh near Tower Pond. Take Mounds Trail to the point where it forks north and south; then leave the trail, heading straight ahead into the marsh with Tower Pond on your left. Provided that water levels and vegetation are favorable, you should spot Black Rail around the edges of the salt pans within 200 yards of the trail.

Driving on from Headquarters Pond, past Picnic Pond, the road enters an extensive sweep of salt marsh. In summer, check the marsh grasses for nesting **Clapper Rail**, **Marsh Wren**, and **Seaside Sparrow**. In the evenings, watch for **Least Bittern** flying over the marsh. Sparrows feed along the roadsides in fall and winter here, most commonly **Savannah** and **Swamp Sparrows**, but occasionally **Clay-colored** and **White-throated**. Sparrows are also plentiful around the lighthouse and in the boat-landing area across the road.

The high observation platform next to the lighthouse overlooks the salt marsh and is one of the best vantage points for spotting **Reddish Egret**. The open, sandy spots in the marsh—salt pans—are excellent spots for plovers and resting shorebirds and waders, particularly during migration. These salt pans are frequented by waders like **Greater** and **Lesser Yellowlegs**, **Willet**, **Whimbrel**, and **Marbled Godwit**. And there is always the possibility of vagrant shorebirds. The uncommon **Buff-breasted** and **Upland Sandpipers** are occasionally seen in the grassy areas surrounding the salt pans. **Wilson's Plover**, numerous during migration, is seen less frequently here in summer. During migrations, scan the hardwood trees and shrubs around the lighthouse for transients; like the Headquarters Pond woods, the lighthouse is another excellent place to bird when weather conditions encourage fallouts.

Lighthouse Pool (6.4 mi.), west of the parking lot, is the most reliable spot year-round for **Marbled Godwit** and, during migrations and winter, for plovers, **Willet**, the abundant **Dunlin**, and other shorebirds. **Least Bitterns** nest in the grassy islands in Lighthouse Pool, as do **Black-necked Stilts** when water conditions suit their needs. The low vegetation along the quarter-mile Levee Trail separating Lighthouse Pool from the bay can be productive in winter for **Song, Swamp,** and **Sharp-tailed Sparrows**—both **Nelson's** and **Saltmarsh** have been seen in the Spartina between the levee and the bay. Winter is also a good time to observe **Common Loon** and **Horned Grebe** bobbing alone in the bay away from the congregations of **Redheads, Greater** and **Lesser Scaups, Buffleheads,** and the infrequent scoters.

Should you arrive at the Refuge immediately following a tropical storm, check the boat landing across the road from the lighthouse for windblown terns. **Common, Bridled,** and **Sooty Terns** have been reported resting on the parking lot here and they can also been seen on the salt pans in the marsh, where gulls and terns tend to congregate after rough weather.

In March 2002, thousands of swallows—primarily **Tree Swallows**—en route to their summer breeding grounds congregated in the Refuge for several days. At dusk, they were observed swarming in a towering, dark, tornado-shaped cloud before coming to roost all at once in the marsh.

Lighthouse Road

Restrooms	At Visitor Center and at Mounds Trail (5.0 mi.).
Off-Highway Parking	At intervals along the road. Parking along roadsides is also permitted.
Birding from Car	Yes
Terrain	Easy along roadsides. Hiking trails are easy but can be wet.
Entrance Fee	$4 per car. Pay fee at Visitor Center. If closed, use self-service kiosk northwest of Center parking lot.
Limited Hours/Days	The Refuge is open daylight hours daily. The Visitor Center is open 8:15 a.m. to 4 p.m. Monday through Friday; 10 a.m. to 5 p.m. on weekends. Closed on Federal holidays.
Permission to Enter	Not required

11 Wakulla Beach Road

A drive down this tranquil dirt road is worth an hour of your time, even if you have scant interest in birds, for it takes you through a lovely forest relatively unmolested by humankind since the virgin pines were logged out. The road runs about four miles from an undeveloped stretch of US 98 through thick woodlands to tiny Wakulla Beach overlooking Goose Creek Bay, a small backwater of Apalachee Bay. The hardwoods along the road teem with insects, making the area especially attractive to migratory and wintering songbirds.

> **From the Florida State Capitol building in Tallahassee (US 27 and FL 61):**
>
> Take FL 61 (South Monroe St.) south. On the south side of town, FL 363 joins FL 61. Stay on FL 363 (Woodville Hwy.) approximately 13 mi. Turn right on US 98, drive 3.4 mi. and turn left on Wakulla Beach Road.
>
> **From the Refuge Visitor Center:**
>
> Return to the intersection of US 98 and CR 59 and turn left. Proceed 9.1 mi. and turn left on Wakulla Beach Road.

The damp woods along the first section of Wakulla Beach Road attract summering hardwood specialists such as **Acadian Flycatcher**, **White-eyed Vireo**, and **Hooded Warbler**. **Yellow-billed Cuckoo**, **Red-eyed Vireo**, and **Northern Parula** summer here as well. In winter, look for **Blue-headed Vireo**, **Golden-crowned Kinglet**, **Yellow-throated Warbler**, and **Black-and-white Warbler**. **Wild Turkey**, **Barred Owl**, and **Blue-gray Gnatcatcher** can be found within sight of the road year-round.

After the first mile, the Florida National Scenic Trail intersects the road, its westerly path tunneling through a shady canopy of hardwoods toward the marsh. This portion of the Florida Trail, as well as the surrounding forests, are open to deer and small-game hunters, so wear bright clothing if you are tempted to venture down the trail during hunting season. And remember your insect repellent: biting insects are numerous here, even in cool weather.

Farther down the road, as the pines begin to predominate, the woods attract **Chuck-will's-widow**, **Eastern Wood-Pewee**, **Yellow-throated Vireo**, and **Summer Tanager**. Just before reaching the beach, the road enters a sparsely populated residential area with old live oaks harboring **Eastern Screech-Owl** and, in winter, the occasional **Whip-poor-will**. During spring migration, these trees—one of the few hardwood stands along the coast—attract incoming warblers and songbirds. In winter, roving flocks of mixed small birds may contain wintering warblers.

The road dead-ends at an unimproved boat landing on Goose Creek Bay. Next to the parking area, the foundations of an early 20th century hotel are now almost obscured by vegetation. Local legend says the hotel burned to the ground prior to its opening and was never rebuilt. In the 50s and 60s,

Goose Creek Bay was well-known as a nightly rest area for enormous numbers of wintering Canada Geese.

On late summer afternoons, watch the thin sliver of beach for the occasional **Yellow-crowned Night-Heron** scampering after fiddler crabs. Looking out over the bay, scan the tops of palm hammocks for **Bald Eagle** nests. In winter, **Horned Grebe**, **Bufflehead**, scoters, and other diving ducks can be observed in the waters offshore.

From the parking area, follow the short westerly path to the point where the woods open onto the marsh, checking the short grasses for **Sedge Wren** (in winter) and longer needlerushes for **Marsh Wren**. The marsh is home to the resident **Seaside Sparrow** and, in winter, to both species of **Sharp-tailed Sparrow**, with **Nelson's** the more numerous by far.

Wakulla Beach Road

Restrooms	No
Off-Highway Parking	Unpaved area at boat landing at end of road. Also at the intersection of the Florida Trail.
Birding from Car	Yes
Terrain	Easy
Entrance Fee	No
Limited Hours/Days	Daylight hours every day of the year
Permission to Enter	Not required

12 Bottoms Road

Bottoms Road winds across a broad salt marsh in the Refuge's Panacea Unit to a small boat landing on Apalachee Bay. It's a fine location for observing a variety of salt marsh bird species. The best times are at dawn and dusk, when a chorus of calls and songs arise from the marsh.

Marsh Wren and **Seaside Sparrow** nest here and it's a popular wintering area for **Sedge Wren**, **Nelson's Sharp-tailed Sparrow**, and **Swamp Sparrow**. Look for the spot where a small creek passes under the road, 1.7 mi. from US 98. At low tide, the sand flats are exposed, and offal discarded by local fish houses attracts **Great Blue Heron**, **Wood Stork**, vultures, and gulls.

As you drive along, check the marsh grasses for rails. **Clapper Rail**, **Virginia Rail** (winter), and **Sora** (winter) are numerous here and most likely to show themselves at high tide. During extreme high tides or when storms flood the marsh, adult rails and chicks seeking higher ground scurry over the roadway in amazing numbers.

In winter, **American Avocet** has been observed in the small ponds along the road. **Short-eared Owls** winter in the marsh as well, though not every year. When present, they can usually be found feeding over the marsh. At dusk, you may also observe them competing for insects with **Northern Harriers** at dusk.

Near the end of the road, check the salt pans for sandpipers. A scope is necessary to look toward Piney Island for the gulls and shorebirds present at low tide. In fall and spring, watch overhead for migrating **White Pelicans**; they occasionally rest on the open water too.

From the Florida State Capitol building in Tallahassee (US 27 and FL 61):

Take FL 61 (South Monroe St.) south approximately 2.5 mi. to the South Monroe St./Gaile Ave. intersection. Turn right on Gaile Ave., proceed a short distance to the traffic light, and turn left on FL 61 (South Adams St./Crawfordville Hwy.) Proceed south to Capital Circle where US 319 joins. Continue south on US 319 (Crawfordville Hwy.) approximately 22 mi. to Medart. At the intersection where US 319 divides from US 98, continue going straight on US 98 for 3 mi. and turn left on Bottoms Road. A small roadside sign 1.1 mi. from US 98 marks the entrance to the Refuge.

From the Refuge Visitor Center:

Return to the intersection of US 98 and CR 59 and turn left. Proceed 19 mi. and turn left on Bottoms Road. The Refuge boundary is 1.1 mi. from US 98.

Shorebirds along the tidal waterways and shoreline are vulnerable to coursing hawks and falcons. Fall migration is a particularly good time to observe these feeding predators—**Sharp-shinned Hawk**, **Cooper's Hawk**, **American Kestrel**, **Merlin**, and **Peregrine Falcon**. Occasional wintering birds can also be seen.

Bottoms Road

Restrooms	No
Off-Highway Parking	At boat landing at end of road. Parking along roadsides permitted
Birding from Car	Yes
Terrain	Easy
Entrance Fee	No
Limited Hours/Days	Daylight hours every day of the year
Permission to Enter	Not required
Notes	The turn-off approximately 2.0 mi. from the US 98 intersection is a private boat landing and cannot be used for parking.

13   Edward Ball Wakulla Springs State Park

In a state where clear natural springs are almost commonplace, Wakulla retains the ability to amaze and enchant every visitor. Every minute of the day, between 100,000 and 400,000 gallons of bracingly cold water flow from the spring's huge blue mouth. The water originates in an aquatic cave system whose origins are unknown, despite sophisticated exploration efforts. Most recently, a research team in 2000 followed the cave more than 18,000 feet from the spring's opening but found no sign of an origination point.

> **From the Florida State Capitol building in Tallahassee (US 27 and FL 61):**
>
> Take FL 61 (South Monroe St.) south approximately 14 mi. (being careful to bear left on FL 61 at 6 mi.) and turn left on FL 267. Proceed ¼ mi. and turn right into the park entrance.

Billed as one of the world's largest and deepest freshwater springs, Wakulla is the main source for the Wakulla River that flows from the Park to the village of St. Marks. A reliable variety of waterbirds can be found roosting, wading, and swimming in its environs.

As you walk down toward the spring, scan the open waters beyond the swimming area for wintering **American Wigeon, Blue-winged Teal,** and **Hooded Merganser.** Check the marshes edging the spring and river for the large herons and egrets, **Purple Gallinule, Common Moorhen, Limpkin,** and **Belted Kingfisher. Double-crested Cormorants** and **Anhingas** can be seen drying their wings high in the cypress trees. Scanning the treeline you may also find **Osprey, Swallow-tailed** and **Mississippi Kites** (both in summer), **Bald Eagle,** and **Red-shouldered Hawk,** most of which nest in the Park.

The 40-minute boat tour down the river (additional fee) affords unusually close observation of **Yellow-crowned Night-Heron, Wood Duck,** and **Purple Gallinule.** Taking the boat tour is the best way to spot **Limpkin,** although these birds aren't seen as frequently as they once were, probably due to a reduction in the population of apple snails, the Limpkin's primary food. The boat will certainly pass close to alligators of all sizes, casually sunning themselves along the riverbanks.

The Nature Walk that begins west of the lodge goes through beech/magnolia hammocks, cypress wetlands, and upland pine forests. Look for **Sharp-shinned Hawk** (fall and winter), **Wild Turkey, Barred Owl, Red-bellied, Downy,** and **Pileated Woodpeckers, Eastern Wood-Pewee** and **Acadian Flycatcher** (both in summer), **Brown-headed Nuthatch, Golden-crowned Kinglet** (winter), **Ruby-crowned Kinglet** (fall through spring), **Blue-gray Gnatcatcher** (fall through spring), **Cedar Waxwing** (winter), **Northern Parula** (spring and summer), **Black-and-white Warbler** (fall through spring), **American Redstart** (spring and fall), **Prothonotary Warbler** (spring and summer), **Hooded Warbler** (summer), **Summer Tanager** (spring and summer), and **Indigo Bunting** (spring).

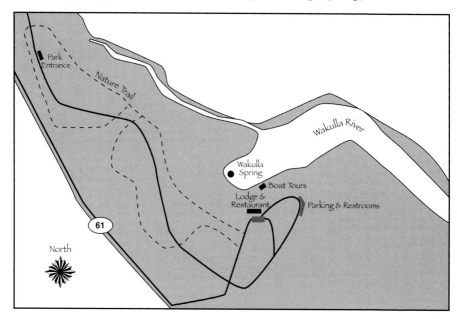

Wakulla Springs State Park

Worth investigating is the Wakulla Springs Lodge, a Mediterranean Revival-style building that found a perfect setting amid the huge live oaks dripping with Spanish moss. The lodge's grand lobby is much the same as it was when constructed in the 1930's, with marble, wrought-iron, and handmade ceramic tile finishes.

Edward Ball Wakulla Springs State Park

Restrooms	Yes
Off-Highway Parking	Yes
Birding from Car	No
Terrain	Easy
Entrance Fee	Standard state park fee
Limited Hours/Days	8 am to sunset daily
Permission to Enter	Not required

Southside Tallahassee

The southern side of Tallahassee offers four excellent birding locations:

14   Black Swamp Nature Preserve (page 38)

15   Robert White Williams Birding Trail (page 40)

16   Thomas P. Smith Water Reclamation Facility (page 42)

17   Southeast Farm Wastewater Reuse Facility (page 44)

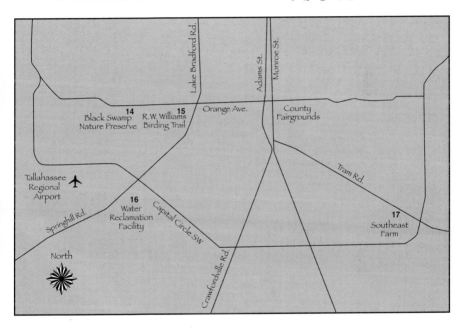

14 Black Swamp Nature Preserve

Black Swamp is considered the last remaining swamp of any size within Tallahassee's city limits. At least 150 species have been reported in the western section of the swamp, including such fall/winter rarities as **Ash-throated Flycatcher**, **Mourning Warbler**, and **Brewer's Blackbird**. Sought-after species such as **Brown Creeper**, **Wilson's Warbler**, and **Rusty Blackbird** have also been observed here.

From the Florida State Capitol building (US 27 and FL 61):

Go south 1.8 mi. on FL 61 (South Monroe St.) to FL 373 (Orange Ave.) and turn right. Go west 2.1 mi. and turn left onto an unmarked road running to the left of a small brick building (a sewer lift station). Park on the grass southeast of the station. (The Florida State University Landscaping Nursery is directly across Orange Ave. from the parking area.)

Unlike most Florida swamps, whose interiors are virtually inaccessible, Black Swamp is intersected by a man-made embankment that zigzags along a power-line easement. This grassy embankment provides easy terrain for walking and unparalleled access to the swamp community. In addition to birds, you might also find otter, fox, beaver, and several frog and turtle species. As of this writing, 25 butterfly species have been identified here.

Although the terrain is flat, the grass-covered embankment can be dew-soaked, so boots are a good idea. Sturdy footwear is advisable for other reasons. Swampland is Cottonmouth habitat, and this poisonous snake may be seen at any time of year, either in the shallow waters along the embankment or crossing the embankment itself. If you encounter Cottonmouth—or any snake—give it a wide berth and continue on your way. The same can be said for the large fire-ant beds dotting the embankment. The mounds are easy to see, but easier to step in when you are more focused on identifying an elusive bird rather than where you put your feet.

From the parking area next to the sewer lift station, walk south toward the metal gate. This gate is usually padlocked, so simply walk around it and continue along the embankment into the swamp. About 100 yards from the gate, the embankment turns left and proceeds for another 200 yards until the power line makes a jog to the right. At this point, the easily walkable portion of the embankment ends, and you should turn around here and retrace your steps.

By late fall or winter, **Song Sparrow**, **Swamp Sparrow**, and five wren species—including **Winter Wren**—can be heard or seen darting about in the emergent grasses, while flocks of **Cedar Waxwings** and **American Robins** forage in the treetops. Fall/winter is the most likely time to spot **Virginia Rail**, last seen in November 1999 hiding among the wet rushes.

The month of March sees the arrival of **Northern Parula**, which, along with the resident **Yellow-throated Warbler**, can often be heard singing high up in the Bald Cypress trees. By April, **Common Yellowthroat** and **Prothonotary Warbler** ("Golden Swamp Warbler") call from the tangled undergrowth. Although seldom encountered, the locally rare **Yellow-crowned Night-Heron** probably nests in Black Swamp and in summer has been observed tending its young. A year-round but irregular visitor is **White-breasted Nuthatch**; Black Swamp lies approximately at the southernmost point of this bird's Florida range.

Especially during July through October, most of Florida's neotropical migrants funnel their way through this swampy corridor, which constitutes probably the most important sanctuary for passerines in Leon County. A watchful birder can also see herons, egrets, **White Ibis, Wood Stork**, and **Limpkin** throughout the year.

Black Swamp Nature Preserve

Restrooms	No
Off-Highway Parking	Yes
Birding from Car	No. Motorized vehicles not allowed in preserve.
Terrain	Easy but can be wet
Entrance Fee	No
Limited Hours/Days	Daylight hours only
Permission to Enter	Not required
Notes	**Mississippi Kite**, a trans-Gulf species not ordinarily seen in peninsular Florida, can often be observed above the parking lot of Harvey's Supermarket, 0.1 mile north of the South Monroe Street-Orange Avenue intersection.

15 Robert White Williams Birding Trail

Williams Trail is a small birding site but a rich one. A grassy track that runs about 500 yards along a tributary of Munson Slough, it is a lush riparian island in a sea of human development. The plant community here is a weedy succession of trees and shrubs offering good cover and plenty of food for passerines. Williams Trail is especially noted for migrant fallouts in April, September, and October.

To avoid birding with the sun in your eyes, bird here just before dawn. At that time, small birds can be roused from the surrounding understory and along the creek bank, including seed-eating sparrows, **Northern Cardinal**, and other finch species. **Red-tailed Hawk** nests near the creek (Keeeeeer!) and **Red-shouldered Hawk** usually makes its presence known ("Keer, Keer, Keer"). In March and April, both hawk species raise young here.

From the Florida State Capitol building (US 27 and FL 61):

Go south 1.8 mi. on FL 61 (South Monroe St.) to FL 373 (Orange Ave.) and turn right. Go west 1.3 mi., cross Springhill Rd. and then a small bridge. At 1.4 mi., turn left into an unpaved open area next to the creek and park on the grass.

From the parking area southward, waders such as **White Ibis**, **Wood Stork**, herons, and egrets can be observed feeding in the creek shallows or flying overhead. During periods of scant rain, the exposed stream bed attracts migrating shorebirds—mostly **Killdeer**, the two yellowlegs species, **Solitary**, **Spotted**, and **Least Sandpiper**, and, during winter, **Wilson's Snipe**—all likely prey for marauding accipiters.

The choicest habitat for warblers and other small birds are the low trees and bushes along the trail. From September through March, one might spot the uncommon **Wilson's Warbler**; **Kentucky Warbler**, which is rare in Leon County, has been reported here in the fall. During migrations, look for **Northern Waterthrush** and numerous **Tennessee**, **Magnolia**, and **Palm Warblers**. Check the clumps of willows along the trail for **Prairie Warbler** and **Yellow Warbler**—the latter arrives here as "early" as late July. Summering warblers include the strikingly beautiful **Hooded Warbler** and **Northern Parula**.

In spring, before departing for their summer nesting grounds, **Cedar Waxwings** gather to feed in the mulberry trees along the trail. **Blue Grosbeak** nests nearby in summer and during migrations **Rose-breasted Grosbeaks** can be heard ("Geek!") or seen in the lower tree branches. By October, countless **Indigo Buntings** seem to be everywhere, confusing birders with their unremarkable fall plumage. In November 2001, a rare Selasphorous hummingbird was reported in the vicinity.

The trail ends at the confluence of the creek and Munson Slough, approximately 500 yards south of the parking area. These secluded waters offer hideaways for **Wood Duck** and the spectacular **Hooded Merganser** (late fall into spring).

The trail is named in honor of the late Robert White Williams, an ornithologist working in this area in the early 20th century, who was the first to compile a comprehensive list of area birds.

Robert White Williams Birding Trail

Restrooms	No
Off-Highway Parking	Yes
Birding from Car	No
Terrain	Easy, but grass on trail can be wet
Entrance Fee	No
Limited Hours/Days	Daylight hours every day of the year
Permission to Enter	Not required

16 Thomas P. Smith Water Reclamation Facility*

Municipal sewage-treatment plants often make prime birding sites, and Tallahassee's main facility is no exception: more than 230 species have been recorded at this site. At any time of year, its four man-made ponds harbor a variety of shorebirds, waders, and waterfowl. Because conditions here are relatively constant, bird populations are less ephemeral than at other birding sites where water levels and food supplies fluctuate.

Aside from the usual efforts to avoid fire ants and other biting insects at this site, one should exercise extreme caution with **Canada Geese** during the breeding season (March). They can be quite aggressive near their nests, which tend to be located—rather inconveniently for birders—on the narrow paths between the treatment ponds. In one confrontation, an angry gander tried to attack the face of an experienced local birder, but the man managed to defend himself with the open end of his scope's tripod. The Canada Geese in Leon County are members of a non-migratory population introduced in the 1960s for hunting purposes. They have taken up residence around many local lakes and are generally considered a nuisance.

Although all treatment ponds are worth a look, the best has traditionally been the easternmost, the farthest from the plant's buildings. In winter, scan the pond waters for a plethora of duck species including **Mallard**, **Blue-winged Teal**, **Northern Shoveler**, **Green-winged Teal**, **Canvasback**, **Redhead**, **Lesser Scaup**, **Bufflehead**, and **Ruddy Duck**. In early 2002, a single immature **Tundra Swan** was observed among the other waterfowl and a **Red-throated Loon** visited briefly. A **Long-tailed Duck** was present the previous winter.

Check the pond edges for **White Ibis** and other waders. **Black-necked Stilt** has been reported here during migrations and **American Avocet** is an occasional visitor between May and January.

> **From the Florida State Capitol building (US 27 and FL 61):**
>
> Go south 1.8 mi. on FL 61 (South Monroe St.) to FL 373 (Orange Ave.) and turn right. Go west 1.4 mi. and turn left on Springhill Rd. Look for the sign on the left marked "City of Tallahassee Water Quality Division" and then turn left into the facility parking area. Enter the building through the right-hand door (as you face the building). You may need to push the admittance button to open the door. Inside, sign in at the front desk; City staff need not be present. Proceed past the front desk and bear left down the hall to the building exit. Once outside, head in the direction of the Purple Martin house, passing between several other buildings to the ponds. When returning, retrace your steps through the building and sign yourself out.

*   *Although this site's official name is Thomas P. Smith Water Reclamation Facility, it is colloquially known as "the Springhill Road sewage treatment facility."*

Greater Yellowlegs, Least Sandpiper, and Long-billed Dowitcher are the dominant wintering shorebird species, but on occasion you might also see Lesser Yellowlegs and Dunlin. Other sandpipers make an appearance during migrations, including Solitary, Semipalmated, Pectoral, Stilt, and Short-billed Dowitcher.

The gull species are represented by Bonaparte's, Herring, and the more numerous Ring-billed. Laughing Gulls appear year-round and the rare Franklin's Gull has turned up in both July and December.

In early fall, look for Eared Grebe. In winter, American Pipit can be seen scampering along the black-rubber banks of the artificial ponds, looking for an insect meal. During migrations, the spray fields next to the ponds attract Dickcissel and Bobolink. Sixteen sparrow species have been recorded on the plant grounds, including Clay-colored, Lark, Grasshopper, Le Conte's, Nelson's Sharp-tailed, and Lincoln's.

Warm weather brings swarms of insects, drawing numerous swallows swooping over the ponds in search of food. During migrations, look for Tree, Bank, Cliff, and Barn Swallows. In summer, the pond environs are inhabited by nesting Northern Rough-winged Swallows.

Thomas P. Smith Water Reclamation Facility

Restrooms	In sign-in building on Springhill Rd. and in Operations and Maintenance Building inside the plant grounds.
Off-Highway Parking	Yes
Birding from Car	No
Terrain	Easy
Entrance Fee	No
Limited Hours/Days	Open all hours every day of the year
Permission to Enter	Not required, but visitors must sign in at building just inside gate (see directions on previous page).

17 Southeast Farm Wastewater Reuse Facility*

This out-of-the-way site is a reliable location for wintering ducks and shorebirds, but it is best known for attracting species rarely seen in this area.

Rarities recorded here in recent years include **Roseate Spoonbill, Ross's Goose** (extremely rare in Florida), **Black-necked Stilt, American Avocet, American Golden-Plover, Franklin's, Thayer's** and **Lesser Black-backed Gulls, Short-eared Owl,** and **Horned Lark.** Three of Leon County's four recorded **Scissor-tailed Flycatchers** since 1971 were spotted in and around the fields on Southeast Farm.

From the Florida State Capitol building (US 27 and FL 61):

Go south 2.5 mi. on FL 61 (South Monroe St.) to CR 259 (Tram Rd.) and turn left. Go east 2.8 mi. and turn right into the facility's gate. Park at the first building on the left, next to the silos.

To access the farm road (see page 45 for access times), drive past the silos, turn right, and enter through the double gate. Bear left to follow the loop.

As you drive from the entrance to the parking area, check the junipers on either side of the road for **Yellow Warbler** (fall). The grounds around the buildings are likely to yield **Eurasian Collared-Dove, Yellow-rumped Warbler** (in typical winter profusion), and **Savannah Sparrow.**

The ponds lie to the west of the building compound and are surrounded by paved walkways. In late fall through winter, scan the waters for ducks such as **Northern Shoveler, Lesser Scaup, Bufflehead,** and **Hooded Merganser.** Joining them in or near the water are **Greater Yellowlegs, Dunlin,** numerous small shorebirds, and **American Pipit.**

In warmer weather, insects flying over the ponds attract swallows—**Tree, Northern Rough-winged, Bank, Cliff,** and **Barn**—the species varying at different times of year. In April, look for **Cave Swallow.**

On the southern side of the ponds, check the bushes and low trees for **Palm Warbler, Yellow Warbler, Savannah Sparrow,** and **Grasshopper Sparrow.** During migrations, hundreds of **American Pipits** may be seen feeding in the close-cropped grasses of the fields south of the ponds. These fields also attract hawks: they are a particularly good location for mature male **Northern Harrier,** which is less frequently seen than females and immature males.

*   *Local birders tend to refer to Southeast Farm by its colloquial name: "the Tram Road sewage treatment facility." It's the site of an ongoing experiment by the City of Tallahassee to make productive use of treated wastewater by irrigating crops—soybeans, corn, canola, and grasses. All of Tallahassee's treated wastewater—some 17 million gallons per day— is recycled in this manner.*

The farm road, which is open to public driving on summer Thursdays, is an eight-mile loop through open fields and woods on the southern side of the facility. In summer, watch the woods for **Yellow-billed Cuckoo, Red-headed** and **Downy Woodpecker, Blue-gray Gnatcatcher, Prairie Warbler, Summer Tanager, Blue Grosbeak,** and **Orchard Oriole.** The fences along the open fields attract **Eastern Kingbird** and **Loggerhead Shrike.** From April through July, **Swallow-tailed** and **Mississippi Kites** hover over the fields, feeding on insects stirred up by irrigation rigs. The spur road heading east from the east side of the farm-road loop is closed to public driving, but the first quarter-mile of this road passes through open woods that have been productive for woodland birds, so it is worthwhile to park and walk down this road to the point where the pine plantation begins. **Scissor-tailed Flycatcher** has been observed here and also in the copse of oaks at the southwest corner of the farm road.

From fall through spring, private vehicles are not allowed on the farm road, but walking along its paved lanes can be quite pleasant in the cooler weather, with opportunities to flush winter sparrows along the way. In winter, **American Kestrels** soar over the fields, occasionally stopping to rest on the fences. During migrations, **Merlin** and **Peregrine Falcon** hunt in the vicinity. Check with the farm supervisor for permission to enter; the gate to the farm road is usually locked, but even if it happens to be open, you should check first before going in, as it might be locked behind you if no one knows you are inside.

Southeast Farm Wastewater Reuse Facility

Restrooms	In plant office
Off-Highway Parking	Yes
Birding from Car	Yes, on the farm roads, when open
Terrain	Easy
Entrance Fee	No
Limited Hours/Days	Ponds: Weekdays 8 a.m. to 4:30 p.m. Farm road: Open to cars on Thursday 8 a.m. to 4:30 p.m. from May 1 to Sept. 1
Permission to Enter	Permission is not required to walk around the ponds or to drive on the farm road during open periods. To walk on the farm road during closed periods, obtain permission from farm supervisor at 850-891-1295.
Notes	When birding the farm fields, stay on the main roadway. Do not walk or drive on irrigated areas, cross fence lines, or open gates. The spur road heading east from the east side of the farm-road loop is closed to public driving but may be accessed on foot. Irrigation sprinklers can spray over the roadway.

Lake Jackson

Lake Jackson is a shallow, 4,000-acre lake surrounded by the low hills of Leon County. It's a popular site for fishing and boating, especially when the water reaches normal levels. Lake Jackson's water levels can be variable—at times full enough to attract bass fishermen and jet skiers, at other times a dry prairie pocketed by a few muddy pools.

Every 25 years or so, water drains from the lake, sometimes quite rapidly, like an emptying bathtub. These natural drawdowns occur during periods of extremely low rainfall when sinkholes in the lake basin—normally clogged with sediments—collapse and open. It can take years for rainfall to replenish the lake. The latest drawdown of Jackson occurred in September 1999 when the area was experiencing a multi-year drought, and water levels remain below normal. What was solid ground in early 2003 may be submerged when you visit. The water levels will to some degree affect the bird species you may expect to see. For example, **Sprague's Pipit** was reported here repeatedly during the winter of 1981-82, when the lake basin was virtually dry.

In recent decades, Lake Jackson's ecosystem has suffered from the development of nearby Tallahassee, and its water quality has been adversely affected by runoff. Still, the lake remains one of the area's premier birding locations and one of the best places to observe migrants, especially in the fall. If you are in the area following a hurricane, be sure to check Lake Jackson for rarities that may have been blown off-course by the storm. A **Magnificent Frigatebird** and a **Sandwich Tern** were seen off Crowder Road Landing following Hurricane Earl in September 1998. **Western Kingbird** is another rarity seen at Crowder Road after heavy weather.

As much of the land surrounding Lake Jackson is private, access for birding purposes is limited to several public boat landings—most of which are situated on the southwest side of the lake. When water levels are low, you may walk from a landing into the lake bed or along the lake's high-water edge, but avoid venturing inland onto private residential property. Driving onto the lake bed is prohibited.

Lake Jackson Mounds State Archaeological Site (small entrance fee) is a non-birding point of interest near Lake Jackson. Located off Crowder Road on Indian Mounds Road, the site was a thriving Native American village from 1100 to 1500. What remains today are several earthen temple mounds that can be ascended via wooden stairways. The Mounds Site is a pleasant spot for a picnic under shady oaks; there are public restrooms and potable water.

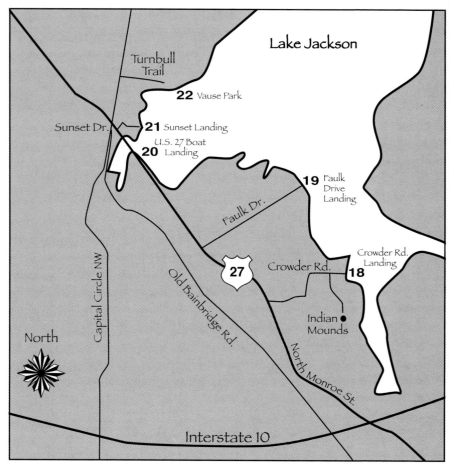

Lake Jackson Birding Spots

Five birding sites are recommended, all on the southwest side of Lake Jackson:

18 Crowder Road Landing (page 50)

19 Faulk Drive Landing (page 52)

20 US 27 Boat Landing (page 55)

21 Sunset Landing (page 56)

22 J. Lee Vause Park (page 57)

If you have time for only one site, make it Faulk Drive Landing. Faulk Drive has the best birding potential in the Lake Jackson area, and during fall/

winter has featured the following rarities: **American White Pelican, Glossy Ibis, Cinnamon Teal, American Avocet** (all four of which are uncommon in the inland Panhandle), **Buff-breasted Sandpiper, White-rumped Sandpiper, Groove-billed Ani, Short-eared Owl, Ash-throated Flycatcher, Vermilion Flycatcher, Nashville Warbler, Wilson's Warbler, Lark Sparrow, Le Conte's Sparrow,** and **Brewer's Blackbird.**

18 Crowder Road Landing

The boat landing at the end of Crowder Road lies near a narrowing of Lake Jackson called Meginnis Arm, offering a close view of the opposite shoreline. The properties surrounding the landing are private. It is permissible to walk along the lake edge—water levels permitting—but avoid venturing onto residential lawns. As with other Lake Jackson birding sites, the species you might encounter depend on lake water levels and recent weather conditions.

> From I-10, take Exit 199 (US 27) and go north on US 27 (toward Havana) 1.7 mi. to Crowder Road. Turn right and follow Crowder Road 1.2 mi. as it winds through a residential area to the paved parking area at the landing.

The offshore waters are good year-round for calling **Pied-billed Grebes**, which nest in the reed shallows in March. Occasionally a wintering **Common Loon** dives for fish farther offshore and in recent years, **American White Pelican**—uncommon inland in North Florida—may be seen foraging there. In January 1995, a male **Cinnamon Teal** was seen near the landing, the first county report since 1893.

Check the shoreline, when existent, for **Killdeer**, waders (herons and egrets), and **Wilson's Snipe** (fall through April). Be alert for various migrating or wintering shorebirds flying about, including the often-elusive migrant **Solitary Sandpiper**. During migrations, look for **Prairie Warbler** and **Yellow Warbler** foraging in the willows near the parking area. Other warblers and choice passerines are likely there during the much longer fall migration (July-October).

The power line over the parking area is a favored perch, offering easy identification of many species, including at least four swallow species—migrant **Tree**, summering **Barn** and **Northern Rough-winged**, and **Purple Martins** (February through summer)—and **Eastern Bluebird**, **House Finch**, and wintering **Eastern Phoebe**. Check dead tree snags in the area for the five common woodpeckers (**Red-headed**, **Red-bellied**, **Downy**, **Northern Flicker**, and **Pileated**) and **Yellow-bellied Sapsucker** (October to March). **Red-winged Blackbirds**, **Common** and **Boat-tailed Grackles**, and **European Starlings** loiter in and around the parking area.

Scan skyward for high-flying birds such as **Osprey**, **Bald Eagle** (fall through winter), **Red-shouldered Hawk** (winter), countless **Ring-billed Gulls**, and lesser numbers of **Herring Gulls** and **Forster's Terns**. Hundreds of wintering **Double-crested Cormorants** may be observed flying over the lake as winter advances.

The private boardwalk to the left of the landing provides sanctuary for resting gulls and terns (and sometimes a stray **Laughing Gull**, which is rare inland). You might also see **Belted Kingfisher**, **Loggerhead Shrike**, and **American Kestrel** perching a discreet distance from the gulls.

Walk up the road for about 500 feet from the landing, checking the shrubs on either side for small woodland birds. With a tape recording, one can induce **Eastern Screech-Owl** to call (August to October). During fall and winter, **Great Horned Owl** "hoo-hoo-hoos" are audible from the pine trees not far off, and **Hermit Thrush** can be heard (though seldom seen) "chucking" in the dense undergrowth along the roadside (fall through April).

Crowder Road Landing

Restrooms	No, but available at nearby Lake Jackson Mounds State Archaeological Site
Off-Highway Parking	Yes
Birding from Car	Yes
Terrain	Easy, but can be muddy
Entrance Fee	No
Limited Hours/Days	No
Permission to Enter	Not required

19 Faulk Drive Landing

Faulk Drive Landing is perhaps more accurately described as a road that dead-ends in a lake. Parking is limited and there are no facilities. Local birders, however, regard the landing and its surroundings as one of the area's most productive sites, due probably to the diversity of habitat.

From I-10:

Take Exit 199 (US 27) and go north on US 27 (toward Havana) for 2.8 mi. Turn right on Faulk Drive.

From Crowder Road:

Return to US 27 and continue north for 1.1 mi. Turn right on Faulk Drive. At 1.3 mi., park in the small turnaround area.

The landing lies on a broad flat of marshy lowland that bulges into the lake. Even when water levels are high, the shoreline tends to be shrubby and poorly defined, which can make for some interesting birding. When water levels are low, it may be tempting to drive beyond the pavement into the dirt tracks around the landing. Be forewarned that mud and deep sand await you.

From the parking area, stroll up the road away from the lake as far as Sanders Rd., scanning the ditches and roadside vegetation for **Eastern Phoebe** (late fall into spring), **White-eyed Vireo**, **Blue-gray Gnatcatcher**, **Common Yellowthroat**, **Eastern Towhee**, and **Common Ground-Dove**. Flocks of up to 16 individuals of the latter have been tallied here. From fall through spring, look also for **House Wren**, **Ruby-crowned Kinglet**, **Wilson's Warbler**, and **White-throated Sparrow**. The rare **Nashville Warbler** has been recorded here in December and January. During migrations, the transient **Prairie Warbler** is easily seen or heard (in spring) along this part of Faulk Drive.

Returning down the road toward the lake, scan the open fields on either side for **Killdeer** and singing flocks of **Bobolink** (April/May) and **Eastern Meadowlark** (October through May). With luck, in winter you might spot a **Vermilion Flycatcher** foraging for insects atop the taller trees. **Eastern Bluebird** and **House Finch** inhabit the sweetgum trees here, as does **American Goldfinch** from November to May. **Brown Thrasher** skulks quietly along the roadsides during the cool months and may be difficult to find, but by spring this bird becomes quite visible and vocal. Icterids—mostly **Red-winged Blackbird**, **Common Grackle**, **Boat-tailed Grackle**, and **Brown-headed Cowbird** (winter)—are plentiful here, distracting the birder from more choice sightings.

During rainy periods, migrating shorebirds stop to inspect water puddles in the fields—**Greater** and **Lesser Yellowlegs**, **Solitary Sandpiper**, **Willet** (rare inland), and **Semipalmated**, **Least**, and **Pectoral Sandpipers** may be seen here. A herd of cattle, slowly advancing through the wet pasture, will flush dozens of **Wilson's Snipe** from the grass.

When unusually heavy rainfall occurs, Lake Jackson inundates the pasture, rising almost to the houses bordering the field. Such conditions attract herons, egrets, ibises, **Wood Storks**, wintering waterfowl, and **American Coots**.

Perched on snags you may find small raptors such as a wintering **American Kestrel**, a rare **Merlin**, or a resident **Cooper's Hawk**, the latter harassed by crows. The larger and more conspicuous **Red-shouldered** and **Red-tailed Hawks** also hunt around the lake. By October, two or three **Northern Harriers** glide low over the fields, preying on rodents. This species—uncommon in North Florida—is more likely to be seen around Lake Jackson than anywhere else in Leon County. Another predatory bird, the **Loggerhead Shrike**, may be observed in pursuit of small birds, dragonflies, and other insect food. In breeding season, shrikes can be seen nurturing their young; it is believed they produce as many as three broods in a season.

As you near the landing, check the weeds and drainage ditch on the left side of the road for wintering **Savannah**, **Song**, and **Swamp Sparrows**, and the rare **Lark Sparrow**. This area also harbors **Sedge** and **Marsh Wren** (in winter when water levels are high) and the resident **Carolina Wren**. **Groove-billed Ani** has been encountered here, as well as **Brewer's Blackbird**. The rare **Ash-throated Flycatcher** has been observed in a stand of willow trees to the left of the landing. This stringy vegetation also attracts **Yellow** and **Prairie Warblers** and many of the common fall warblers. **American Bittern** is occasionally seen in the mudflat grasses near the water.

Numerous **Tree** and **Barn Swallows** migrate quickly through the Lake Jackson area, as do fewer numbers of **Snow Geese**, **Sandhill Cranes**, **Purple Martins** and **Bank Swallows**. **Turkey Vultures** and **Ospreys** are mainstays overhead, and adult and immature **Bald Eagles** are being recorded here in increasing numbers (fall into spring).

In winter the waters off Faulk Drive Landing occasionally attract hundreds of **Double-crested Cormorants**, countless **Ring-billed Gulls**, and lesser numbers of **Herring Gulls** and **Forster's Terns**. Rafts of 100 or more **Pied-billed Grebes** feed in the lake, along with a few **Horned Grebes** and the occasional **Common Loon**. **Pied-billed Grebes** nest along the grassy stretches of shoreline, and floating strands of water lilies and lotus lilies harbor the nests of **Purple Gallinules** (absent in winter) and **Common Moorhens**. The **American White Pelican**, although still a rarity in these parts, has been observed here with increasing frequency, even in summer.

In the water a few yards off the landing is Porter Hole Sink, the primary sinkhole through which lakewater drains when Lake Jackson undergoes one of its periodic drawdowns. During the September 1999 drawdown, local people gathered at Faulk Drive Landing to watch the last of Jackson's water swirl into the sinkhole. Even if water levels are low, resist the temptation to venture into the sinkhole area—there are numerous secondary holes and walking there is unsafe.

Faulk Drive Landing

Restrooms	No
Off-Highway Parking	Yes
Birding from Car	Yes
Terrain	Roadsides are easy but lake bed has mud and deep sand.
Entrance Fee	No
Limited Hours/Days	No
Permission to Enter	Not required

20 US 27 Boat Landing

On warm weekends, this sandy spot just off US 27 is a favorite launching spot for boaters. A broad expanse of Lake Jackson is viewable from here.

A variety of waders and waterbirds can be observed in the waters around the landing. In winter, look for **Common Loon, Horned Grebe, Ring-necked Duck**, scaup, and **Ruddy Duck**. Year-round you may find **Anhinga**, herons and egrets, **Wood Stork, Osprey, Bald Eagle, Common Moorhen**, and **American Coot**.

From I-10:

Take Exit 199 (US 27) and go north on US 27 (toward Havana) for 3.8 mi.

From Faulk Drive:

Return to US 27 and continue north for 1.0 mi.

Turn right into landing parking area.

Gray Catbird and Orchard Oriole nest in the shrubs east of the parking area, and in summer, **Least Bittern** has been observed in the dog fennel along the lakeshore. During migrations, **Yellow** and **Prairie Warbler** can be found in the willows around the landing. Recently recorded rarities at this site include **Greater White-fronted Goose** and **Field Sparrow**, both observed in late winter.

Across US 27 lies Little Lake Jackson, a reliable spot for **Purple Gallinule** (spring through fall), although there is nowhere to park and heavy traffic along the highway can preclude a safe crossing on foot.

US 27 Boat Landing

Restrooms	Portable unit
Off-Highway Parking	Yes
Birding from Car	Yes
Terrain	Easy
Entrance Fee	No
Limited Hours/Days	Daylight hours
Permission to Enter	Not required

21 Sunset Landing

This boat landing on the western shore of Lake Jackson may have earned its name from fishermen coming in after a day on the lake. Cleaning their catch at the nearby Red and Sam's Fish Camp, fishermen are regularly joined by a few **Black-crowned Night-Herons** hoping to scavenge the odd scrap. The fresh fish offal may also account for the presence of a **Brown Pelican**, which wandered inland and has been content to stay. This coastal bird has been observed swimming in the waters off Sunset Landing.

In past years, the threatened **Least Tern** has nested successfully on mudflats around Lake Jackson and has foraged off Sunset Landing where, by July and August, they can be seen feeding their fledglings in preparation for migration. (Least Terns have nested in Leon County since 1955. These birds, along with those confirmed in Hamilton County, are the only nesting populations reported inland in North Florida. In April, Least Tern may be observed nesting on the rooftops of certain Tallahassee supermarkets.)

From I-10:

Take Exit 199 (US 27) and go north on US 27 (toward Havana) for 4.6 mi. Turn right on CR 361 (Old Bainbridge Road).

From Faulk Drive:

Continue north on US 27 for 1.8 mi. and turn right on CR 361 (Old Bainbridge Road).

Proceed 0.05 mi. to Jackson Cove Rd. and turn right. At the Dead End sign (0.3), turn left and follow the road, pass the small restaurant on the right, to the public parking area just past the Sunset Boat Landing sign.

From Sunset Landing's parking area, look across the landing, scanning the trees and shrubs for **Eastern Phoebe**, **Loggerhead Shrike**, and **Eastern Meadowlark**. The wooded area behind the restrooms provides cover for vireos, warblers, and gnatcatchers.

When water levels remain low, dog fennel grows in the lake bed close to shore, providing excellent habitat for sparrows, notably **Swamp Sparrow**. The open areas here offer good views of **Savannah Sparrow**.

Sunset Landing

Restrooms	Yes
Off-Highway Parking	Yes
Birding from Car	Yes
Terrain	Easy
Entrance Fee	No
Limited Hours/Days	No
Permission to Enter	Not required
Notes	Picnic tables near public parking area

22 J. Lee Vause Park

This county park of mostly open, undulating fields rolls down to the western shore of Lake Jackson. The park is designed primarily for large gatherings that require wide open spaces; however, Leon County has made an effort to preserve the native vegetation where possible and to add landscape plants that produce food for wildlife.

From the park entrance, bear to the right and follow the road to the parking area. Park in the parking area next to the picnic pavilions (0.3 mi.), and walk through the live oak and sweetgum woods to the raised boardwalk skirting the lake edge. This wooded area attracts **Barred Owl**, woodpeckers, **Chipping Sparrow**, **White-throated Sparrow**, and **American Goldfinch**. From the boardwalk, scan the marshy margins of the lake for herons, **Purple Gallinule**, and **Common Moorhen**.

From I-10:

Take Exit 199 (US 27) and go north on US 27 (toward Havana) for 4.6 mi. Turn right on CR 361 (Old Bainbridge Road) and proceed 0.3 mi. to park entrance (Marjorie Turnbull Trail) on the right.

From Sunset Landing:

Return to Old Bainbridge Road and continue 0.2 mi. to park entrance (Marjorie Turnbull Trail) on the right.

J. Lee Vause Park

Restrooms	Yes
Off-Highway Parking	Yes
Birding from Car	Yes
Terrain	Easy
Entrance Fee	No
Limited Hours/Days	8 a.m. to sunset
Permission to Enter	Not required
Notes	Picnic area

Central Tallahassee

Tallahassee's central area offers three birding locations:

23 San Luis Mission Park (page 60)

24 Myers Park (page 62)

25 The Pond at Church's Chicken (page 63)

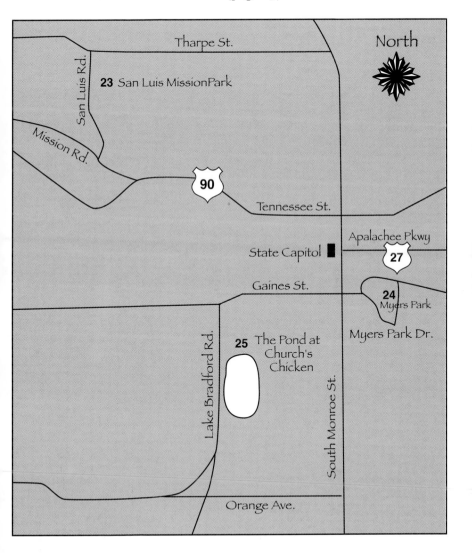

23 San Luis Mission Park

San Luis Mission Park lies in a low basin in suburban northwest Tallahassee. A typical city facility with play areas and picnic tables, the 70-acre park is heavily wooded, offering attractive habitat to birds who favor damp riparian woods. More than 150 species have been reported here. The most interesting birding can be found by strolling around Lake Esther, a small, shallow pond near the parking area. A boardwalk crossing the lake's eastern side provides good views of the water and the swampy area adjacent to the lake.

> **From the Florida State Capitol building (US 27 and FL 61):**
>
> Go north 1.8 mi. on US 27 (North Monroe St.) to Tharpe St. and turn left. Go west 2 mi. and turn left on San Luis Rd. Proceed 0.2 mi. and turn left into the park entrance. Follow the drive a short distance to the parking area.

A local birder posts a current list of the park's birds on a bulletin board outside the restrooms. A few steps away is the boardwalk where you can begin a circuit of the lake. As you pass through the stand of willows overhanging the boardwalk, look for **Yellow Warbler** (fall) and **Prairie Warbler** (spring and fall). The uncommon **Wilson's Warbler** was also reported in these willows during the winter of 2000-2001. The bird list reports 28 species of warblers at San Luis Mission Park.

The midsection of the boardwalk offers a fine vantage point for close viewing of wintering ducks, **Belted Kingfisher**, **White Ibis**, herons, and egrets. **Green Heron** can be seen here year-round, particularly in summer. Before moving on, turn your back to the lake and check the trees for **Barred Owl**, **Broad-winged Hawk** (April into October), and **Pileated Woodpecker**. Look also for **Eastern Bluebirds** nesting in tree-hole cavities.

After exiting the boardwalk, turn right and follow the lake edge to a trail that continues into the lakeside woods. **Red-shouldered Hawks** nest in the trees here and can be seen year-round, along with **Red-bellied** and **Downy Woodpeckers**. **Northern Flicker** is present from October through March. In summer, look for **Great Crested Flycatcher** and **Northern Parula**.

San Luis Mission Park

Restrooms	Yes
Off-Highway Parking	Yes
Birding from Car	No
Terrain	Easy
Entrance Fee	No
Limited Hours/Days	Daylight hours every day of the year.
Permission to Enter	Not required
Note	The best birding in San Luis Park usually occurs on weekdays, when it is less crowded.

Five species of vireo have been recorded in San Luis Park: **Blue-headed** (November through March), **Philadelphia** (September and October, though rarely), **Red-eyed** (spring, August and September), **White-eyed** (May through October), and **Yellow-throated** (March into October). The best place for viewing them is on or near the boardwalk.

24 Myers Park

One of Tallahassee's oldest city parks, Myers Park is a 16-acre preserved woodland in the center of town, just a few blocks from the State Capitol.

Park in the lots anywhere along Myers Park Dr. and wander down into the park, away from the recreational areas. The center of the park is a shady ravine where you can pick up an exercise trail that runs through tall oaks, magnolia, and mature pine. A brush-lined creek flows through the bottom of the ravine.

From the Florida State Capitol building:

Go east 0.6 mi. on US 27 (Apalachee Parkway) to Broward Dr. and turn right. Go one block to Lafayette Dr. and continue straight onto Myers Park Dr. The park begins on your right. At the stop sign, bear right and park in any of the lots to the right along Myers Park Dr.

Look for **Broad-winged Hawk** (spring through fall), **Barred Owl**, woodpeckers, **Yellow-throated Vireo** (spring through fall), and **White-breasted Nuthatch**. The park also attracts migrant species, particularly in fall. Spring migrants are possible, though not as reliably as in coastal areas.

Myers Park

Restrooms	Yes
Off-Highway Parking	Yes
Birding from Car	Yes
Terrain	Easy
Entrance Fee	No
Limited Hours/Days	Weekdays, sunrise to sunset
Permission to Enter	Not required

25 The Pond at Church's Chicken

At the time of this writing, this recently created holding pond just south of Florida State University had begun attracting the notice of Tallahassee birders. Interest in the new site rose perceptibly in early February 2002, when a lone **Red-throated Loon** in winter plumage was observed floating among the usual **Pied-billed Grebes** and ducks.

> **From the Florida State Capitol building (US 27 and FL 61):**
>
> Go south 0.2 mi. on FL 61 (South Monroe St.) to Gaines St. and turn right. Go west 1.3 mi. and turn left on Lake Bradford Rd. Proceed 0.3 mi. and turn left into the park entrance.

A walking/bike trail encircles the pond, offering a nice vantage point of the pond waters at any time of day. Simply move around the trail until the sun is out of your eyes, and look for wintering **Ring-necked Duck, Hooded Merganser, Bufflehead, Lesser Scaup, Northern Shoveler**, and **Common Goldeneye**.

The southern end of the pond tends to offer the best birding. From the parking area, walk south along the street side, checking grassy areas at the pond edge for **Wilson's Snipe**. The chain-link fence marking the southern border of the property offers perches for **Little Blue Heron, Loggerhead Shrike**, and **American Kestrel**. Groups of **White Ibis** often gather at the southern end of the pond.

The woodland edges on the opposite side of the pond from the parking area offer choice habitat for small passerines such as kinglets, vireos, warblers, and wintering sparrows. **Wood Stork** and **Bald Eagle**, both more commonly found outside the city, may occasionally be seen circling over the pond, the latter scattering the flocks of **Ring-billed Gulls** congregating along the trail.

The Pond at Church's Chicken

Restrooms	No
Off-Highway Parking	Yes
Birding from Car	Yes
Terrain	Easy
Entrance Fee	No
Limited Hours/Days	Daylight hours every day of the year
Permission to Enter	Not required
Note	Future plans call for connecting the trail encircling the pond to the St. Marks Hiking/Biking Trail that leads from Tallahassee to the fishing hamlet of St. Marks.

North of Tallahassee

Two birding locations are found north of Tallahassee:

26 Alfred B. Maclay Gardens State Park (page 66)

27 Henry M. Stevenson Memorial Bird Trail at Tall Timbers Research Station (page 69)

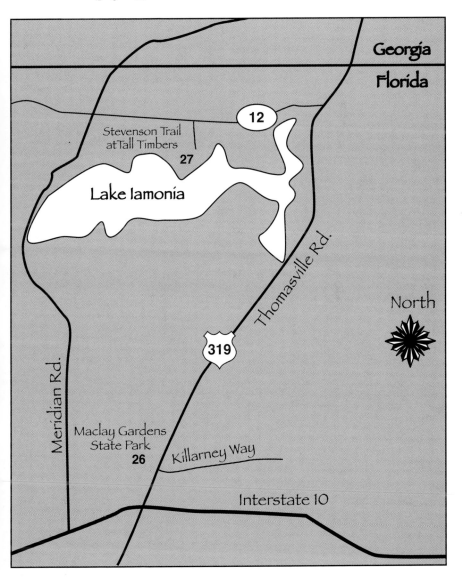

26 Alfred B. Maclay Gardens State Park

The ornamental gardens, developed in the 1920s and 30s by New York financier Alfred Maclay and later by his widow Louise, form the centerpiece of this tranquil and accessible state park. Massive pines and live oaks create a high canopy ringing with songbird notes and woodpecker calls. Down below, the shrubs and smaller trees provide good cover for songbirds.

> **From I-10:**
>
> Take Exit 203 (US 319/ Thomasville Rd.) and go north approximately 1 mi. to Killarney Way. Turn left into the park entrance.

The park is not known for attracting rarities, perhaps because it is not as frequently birded as other Tallahassee sites. However, it is worth a stop for the novice birder because many of the species commonly found in this area can be observed here.

The ranger station at the entrance has maps of the gardens and Lake Overstreet hiking trails and may also have a bird list. From the station, drive 0.2 mi. and turn right on the first paved road to the Lake Hall recreation area. Views of the water are limited here by thick lakeside vegetation, but the woodlands along the road and parking area are good for **Barred Owl**, **White-eyed Vireo**, **Red-eyed Vireo** (summer), **Ruby-crowned Kinglet** (winter), warblers—**Yellow-rumped** (winter), **Yellow-throated**, **Pine**, and **Black-and-white** (winter)—and **Song** and **White-throated Sparrows** (winter).

From the parking area, walk beyond the picnic pavilion where a stand of enormous pines, oaks, and sweet gums offers habitat for **Red-bellied Woodpecker**, **Yellow-bellied Sapsucker** (winter), **Downy Woodpecker**, **Northern Flicker**, **White-breasted Nuthatch**, and **Northern Parula** (summer). In late winter, the sweetgums attract **Cedar Waxwings** as they prepare for migration to their northern breeding grounds.

From Lake Hall, return to the main road, turn right, and proceed 0.5 mi. to the gardens parking area. A map is helpful for wandering the network of garden paths, but if time is limited, just walk the wide, brick-paved drive running from the gardens entrance to the Maclay House, the former owners' summer retreat. In the canopy overhead, look for pairs of **Summer Tanagers** scolding **Fish Crows** away from their territories. Stroll a short distance down the drive to a small pavilion overlooking Lake Hall where in winter you may see **Horned Grebe** and ducks. **Ring-necked, Lesser Scaup,** and **Ruddy** are the common duck species here; **American Wigeon, Bufflehead,** and **Red-breasted Merganser** are observed less often.

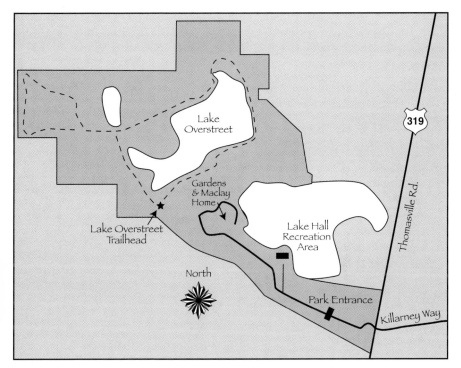

Maclay Gardens State Park

Also in winter, scan the shoreline for **Wilson's Snipe**, **Swamp Sparrow** and for **Belted Kingfisher** resting between fishing excursions on low, overhanging branches. **Pied-billed Grebe**, **Common Moorhen**, and **Purple Gallinule** (spring through fall) putter among the aquatic vegetation. **Common Loons** inhabit the lake in winter, and **Red-shouldered Hawks** may be seen around the lake throughout the year. In summer, listen for their "keer, keer, keer."

At the Maclay House, look for **Eastern Bluebirds** on the lawn sloping down to the lake. In winter, check the bushes in the gardens for **Ruby-crowned Kinglets** and **Yellow-rumped Warblers**—both plentiful—and for **American Robins** dining on berries produced by the garden's shrubs.

The road to the Lake Overstreet trail head is 0.1 mi. past the gardens parking area. The trail is a three-mile circuit of pristine Lake Overstreet; look for **Osprey**, waterfowl, and wading birds. Another option is the 1.5-mile Ravine Trail, accessed by taking the same trail head and turning left (west) at Gum Pond. The Ravine Trail takes you through sloping hills and ravines in a mixed pine-hardwood forest. Winter birds visible from the trails include **Bald Eagle**, **American Woodcock**, and **Hermit Thrush**. In summer, look for **Yellow-billed Cuckoo** and **Summer Tanager**; listen at dusk for **Chuck-will's-widow**. Year-round residents are **Red-tailed** and **Red-shouldered Hawks, Great Horned Owl, Loggerhead Shrike**, and **Eastern Towhee**.

Adjoining the park to the west across Meridian Rd. is the Elinor Klapp-Phipps City Park with extensive woodland trails looping to the edge of Lake Jackson.

Alfred B. Maclay Gardens State Park

Restrooms	At Lake Hall recreation area and at entrance to gardens
Off-Highway Parking	Yes
Birding from Car	Yes
Terrain	Easy
Entrance Fee	Standard state park fee
Limited Hours/Days	Daily from 8 a.m. to sunset
Permission to Enter	Not required

27 Henry M. Stevenson Memorial Bird Trail at Tall Timbers Research Station

The half-mile trail follows a path frequently birded by Dr. Henry M. Stevenson, the late Florida ornithologist who held a research fellowship at Tall Timbers. It begins at the edge of an open field high on a hill overlooking Lake Iamonia and carries you down through a mature mixed-pine forest to a secluded pond where Tall Timbers has erected a cabin with a bird window.

Specialties of the Stevenson Bird Trail are **Hairy Woodpecker**, **White-breasted Nuthatch**, **Yellow-breasted Chat**, and **Bachman's Sparrow** (the latter two in summer). A generally reliable observation spot for **White-breasted Nuthatch** is the bird window at the cabin.

> **From the intersection of I-10 Exit 203 and Thomasville Rd (US 319):**
>
> Go north 13.3 mi. to CR 12 and turn left. Continue 2.7 mi. and turn left into the station entrance on Henry Beadle Dr. Follow the signs to the Komarek Science Education Center. Park and check in (mandatory) at the Center for directions to the trail.

Year-round residents you are likely to see along the trail are **Northern Bobwhite**, **Cooper's Hawk**, **Red-headed Woodpecker**, **Pileated Woodpecker**, **Brown-headed Nuthatch**, **Pine Warbler**, and **Field Sparrow**. Less likely but still present is **Wild Turkey**.

In summer, look for **Eastern Wood-Pewee**, **Eastern Kingbird**, **Yellow-throated Vireo**, **Yellow-throated Warbler**, **Northern Parula**, **Summer Tanager**, **Blue Grosbeak**, **Indigo Bunting**, and **Orchard Oriole**. As you walk down the trail toward the cabin, listen for the call of a **Red-shouldered Hawk** soaring over Lake Iamonia.

Green Heron and **Purple Gallinule** (spring through fall) are common sights at Gannet Pond. In spring and summer, check the hardwoods around the edge of the pond for **Red-eyed Vireo**, **Wood Thrush**, and **Prothonotary**, **Kentucky**, and **Hooded Warblers**. Inside the cabin, the comfortable wicker seats at the bird window give you the opportunity for close observation of birds visiting the feeders as well as wading birds foraging around the pond.

Winter sparrows commonly seen along the trail include **Chipping**, **Field**, **Savannah**, **Song**, **Swamp**, and **White-throated**. **White-crowned** and **Fox Sparrows** and **Dark-eyed Junco** are occasionally reported.

Tall Timbers does research to further understanding about land-management practices that preserve wildlife habitat and conserve the land itself. Guided walks with a staff ornithologist or naturalist are available by appointment.

Henry M. Stevenson Memorial Bird Trail at Tall Timbers Research Station

Restrooms	In the Komarek Science Education Center
Off-Highway Parking	Yes
Birding from Car	No
Terrain	Moderate
Entrance Fee	No
Limited Hours/Days	Weekdays, 8 a.m. to 4:30 p.m. Other hours by prior arrangement only: call 850-893-4153, ext 251.
Permission to Enter	Mandatory. Check in at Komarek Science Education Center.

List of Florida Birds
&
Their Status in the Tallahassee Region

(New AOU names and sequence)

Numbers to the left of the bird's name refer to months of the year; letters refer to the weeks of the month, with the 29th through the 31st days included under "d." Parentheses surrounding these symbols indicate a single occurrence over a long period of time.

Other symbols are the following:

+	one or more records outside the stated extremes, but species not expected then
res.	permanent resident
v.	irregular visitor at any time of the year
?	status not well understood
*	largely or entirely confined to the coast

For species not known to occur in the Tallahassee Region, capital letters show where they may be expected:

E	the east coast
O	offshore
NE	northeastern Florida
P	peninsular Florida
S	southern Florida
SE	southeastern Florida

Horizontal lines separate families and some subfamilies.

Editor's Note: *This list was compiled by Dr. Henry M. Stevenson in the form of a field card prior to his death in 1991. Since then, the status of a few birds has changed and new birds have been observed in this area. To reflect the most important changes, we have updated the list where appropriate. Our status revisions to Dr. Stevenson's original field card are shown in italics.*

Status	Species
	* Loon, _Red-throated_
10-5+	* " , Common
res.	Grebe, Pied-billed
9d-6d	" , Horned
11-3	* " , Red-necked
11-4	" , Eared
P	" , Western
O	* Shearwater,
O	* Storm-Petrel,
O	* Booby,
11-5+	* Gannet, Northern
9-7	Pelican, American White
res.	* " , Brown
11-2	Cormorant, Great
res.	" , Double-crested
res.	Anhinga
4b-11b+	* Frigatebird, Magnificent
9a-5b+	Bittern, American
3b-10c+	" , Least
res.	Heron, Great Blue
res.	Egret, Great
res.	" , Snowy
res.	Heron, Little Blue
res.	" , Tricolored
3-12	* Egret, Reddish
3-11+	" , Cattle
res.	Heron, Green
res.	Night-Heron, Black-crowned
res.	" , Yellow-crowned
res.	Ibis, White
Miami	" , Scarlet
res.	" , Glossy
4b-c	" , White-faced
5-10+	* Spoonbill, Roseate
3b-12b+	Stork, Wood
res.	Vulture, Black
res.	" , Turkey
v.	* Flamingo, Greater
3-5; 10-1	Whistling-Duck, Fulvous
10a-3a	Goose, Greater White-fronted
10a-4a+	" , Snow
res.	" , Canada
11c-3a	Swan, Tundra
res.	Duck, Wood
10a-6a+	Gadwall
10d-3a+	Wigeon, Eurasian
9d-7b+	" , American
9b-6c+	Duck, American Black
res.	Mallard
3-12	Duck, Mottled
8a-6b+	Teal, Blue-winged
9a-6b+	Shoveler, Northern
P	Pintail, White-cheeked
9a-6a+	" , Northern

Status	Species
10b-6a+	Teal, Green-winged
10d-4d+	Canvasback
10a-7c	Redhead
10-5+	Duck, Ring-necked
10d-7a	* Scaup, Greater
10c-8a+	" , Lesser
	* Eider,
E	* Duck, Harlequin
11c-3a	" , Long-tailed
10d-6d	* Scoter, Black
10d-6d+	* " , Surf
10d-6a	* " , White-winged
11b-4b+	Goldeneye, Common
11a-5a+	Bufflehead
10d-4c+	Merganser, Hooded
12a-5a	" , Common
10-8+	" , Red-breasted
12c	Duck, Masked
10c-5a+	" , Ruddy
res.	Osprey
2d-8c	Kite, Swallow-tailed
	" ,
4b-9a+	" , Mississippi
8b-6b+	Eagle, Bald
8c-5c+	Harrier, Northern
8-6+	Hawk, Sharp-shinned
res.	" , Cooper's
res.	" , Red-shouldered
3d-10d+	" , Broad-winged
4-7	" , Short-tailed
10-1	" , Swainson's
res.	" , Red-tailed
?	" , Rough-legged
10-3	Eagle, Golden
P	Caracara, Crested
res.	Kestrel, American
9b-4d+	Merlin
9b-5b	Falcon, Peregrine
res.	Turkey, Wild
res.	Bobwhite, Northern
9d-5d	Rail, Yellow
3b-12b	" , Black
res.	" , Clapper
res.	" , King
9a-5b+	" , Virginia
8d-5d	Sora
3-10+	Gallinule, Purple
res.	Moorhen, Common
res.	Coot, American
res.	Limpkin
res.	Crane, Sandhill
res.	Plover, Black-bellied
3-5; 8-12+	Golden-Plover, American
res.	Plover, Snowy

Status	Species	Status	Species
res.	Plover, Wilson's	res.	* Tern, Royal
res.	" , Semipalmated	3d-12b+	* " , Sandwich
7b-6a	" , Piping	Keys	* " , Roseate
res.	Killdeer	4-10+	* " , Common
res.	* Oystercatcher, American	res.	" , Forster's
3-9	* Stilt, Black-necked	4a-9d+	* " , Least
v.	* Avocet, American	8d, 9d	* " , Bridled
res.	Yellowlegs, Greater	4-6; 9-10	* " , Sooty
7a-6a+	" , Lesser	4c-11b+	" , Black
3-5; 7-10	Sandpiper, Solitary	Keys	* Noddy, Brown
res.	Willet	res.	* Skimmer, Black
7a-6b+	Sandpiper, Spotted	E	* Dovekie
3-5;7-9+	" , Upland	res.	Dove, Rock
res.?	* Whimbrel	Keys	* Pigeon, White-crowned
v.	* Curlew, Long-billed	*res.*	*Collared-Dove, Eurasian*
5d	Godwit, Hudsonian	4-5; 10-1+	Dove, White-winged
res.?	* " , Marbled	res.	" , Mourning
res.	* Turnstone, Ruddy	res.	Ground-Dove, Common
7d-6b+	* Knot, Red	St. Pete	Budgerigar
res.	* Sanderling	Miami	Parakeet, Canary-w.
4-10+	Sandpiper, Semipalmated	4-5; 8-10	Cuckoo, Black-billed
6c-5a	" , Western	4a-11c+	" , Yellow-billed
7b-5d+	" , Least	11b	* " , Mangrove
4d-6b+	" , White-rumped	S	Ani, Smooth-billed
3b; 8a-10a	" , Baird's	9d-1a	" , Groove-billed
3-5; 7-11+	" , Pectoral	res.	Owl, Barn
10d-1d	" , Purple	res.	Screech-Owl, Eastern
9b-6b+	Dunlin	res.	Owl, Great Horned
3-5; 7-10+	Sandpiper, Stilt	10d-11b	" , Burrowing
4-5; 8-10	" , Buff-breasted	res.	" , Barred
4b	Ruff	10d-4a	" , Short-eared
res.	* Dowitcher, Short-billed	4a-10c+	Nighthawk, Common
8-4+	" , Long-billed	3-10a+	Chuck-will's-widow
8-5+	Snipe, Wilson's	8d-5a	Whip-poor-will
res.?	Woodcock, American	3c-11b	Swift, Chimney
3,6; 7-10+	Phalarope, Wilson's	12c-3a	" , Vaux's
5b-d; 12d	* " , Red-necked	2c-11a+	Hummingbird, Ruby-throated
11-12; 5	* " , Red	*11*-4a	" , Rufous
9a	* Jaeger, Pomarine	*11c-4+*	" , *Black-chinned*
v.	* " , Parasitic	res.	Kingfisher, Belted
res.	Gull, Laughing	res.	Woodpecker, Red-headed
v.	" , Franklin's	res.	" , Red-bellied
E	" , Little	10a-4d	Sapsucker, Yellow-bellied
(8b-d)	" , Common Black-headed	res.	Woodpecker, Downy
10d-5b+	" , Bonaparte's	res.	" , Hairy
res.	" , Ring-billed	res.	" , Red-cockaded
res.	" , Herring	res.	Flicker, Northern
St. Pete	" , Thayer's	res.	Woodpecker, Pileated
v.	" , Lesser Black-backed	5d; 9b-10a	Flycatcher, Olive-sided
P	* " , Iceland	4a-11b+	Wood-Pewee, Eastern
4-5	* " , Glaucous	4a-10d	Flycatcher, Acadian
10c-1a	* Kittiwake, Black-legged	5; 9-10	" , Least
4-10	* Tern, Gull-billed		" ,
res.	* " , Caspian	9d-4c+	Phoebe, Eastern

Status	Species
9d-3d+	Flycatcher, Vermilion
?	" , *Ash-throated*
3c-9d+	" , Great Crested
4-5; 9-12+	Kingbird, Western
3b-10d	" , Eastern
4a-10b+	" , Gray
9-1, 3-6	Flycatcher, Scissor-tailed
res.	Shrike, Loggerhead
res.	Vireo, White-eyed
9b-10c	" , Bell's
10a-4d	" , Blue-headed
3b-10+	" , Yellow-throated
4c; 10d	" , Warbling
4-5; 9-10	" , Philadelphia
3b-11b+	" , Red-eyed
4b-7b	" , Black-whiskered
res.	Jay, Blue
P	" , Scrub
res.	Crow, American
res.	" , Fish
10-12	Lark, Horned
1d-10d+	Martin, Purple
7c-6a	Swallow, Tree
Keys	" , Bahaman
3a-1c	" , No. Rough-winged
4-5; 8-10+	" , Bank
4-5; 8-10+	" , Cliff
12d; 3a	" , Cave
3c-12a+	" , Barn
res.	Chickadee, Carolina
res.	Titmouse, Tufted
10a-5b	Nuthatch, Red-breasted
res.	" ,White-breasted
res.	" ,Brown-headed
10c-3d	Creeper, Brown
Miami	Bulbul, Red-whiskered
res.	Wren, Carolina
10a-3d+	" , Bewick's
9c-4d+	" , House
10b-4c+	" , Winter
9c-5b+	" , Sedge
res. *	" , Marsh
10c-4a+	Kinglet, Golden-crowned
9d-5a	" , Ruby-crowned
res.	Gnatcatcher, Blue-gray
res.	Bluebird, Eastern
4-5; 8-10+	Veery
4-5; 9-10+	Thrush, Gray-cheeked
4-5; 9-10+	" , Swainson's
10b-4d	" , Hermit
3d-11a	" , Wood
res.	Robin, American
9b-5b+	Catbird, Gray
res.	Mockingbird, Northern

Status	Species
res.	Thrasher, Brown
res.	Starling, European
SE	Myna, Hill
10b-5b+	Pipit, Water
10c-4b	" , Sprague's
10c-5d+	Waxwing, Cedar
4; 8-10+	Warbler, Blue-winged
4; 8-10+	" , Golden-winged
4-5; 9-11+	" , Tennessee
10a-4d	" , Orange-crowned
3b; 9c-10b+	" , Nashville
2d-11b+	Parula, Northern
4-5; 7-10+	Warbler, Yellow
4-5; 8-10+	" , Chestnut-sided
4-5; 9-11+	" , Magnolia
4-5; 9-10+	" , Cape May
4-5; 9-11+	" , Black-throated Blue
10b-5b+	" , Yellow-rumped
11a-1a; 4c	" , Black-throated Gray
3-5; 9-11+	" , Black-throated Green
4-5; 8-10+	" , Blackburnian
res.	" , Yellow-throated
res.	" , Pine
E	" , Kirtland's
3-5; 7-11+	" , Prairie
9b-5b	" , Palm
4-5; 10-11	" , Bay-breasted
4-5; 9-11+	" , Blackpoll
4-5; 7-9+	" , Cerulean
7c-5b+	" , Black-and-White
3-5; 7-11+	Redstart, American
3b-10c	Warbler, Prothonotary
4-5; 8-10+	" , Worm-eating
3c-10c	" , Swainson's
8b-5d	Ovenbird
3-5; 8-11+	Waterthrush, Northern
2c-10c+	" , Louisiana
3d-10b+	Warbler, Kentucky
5b-d; 9c, d	" , Connecticut
8d-9d	" , Mourning
res.	Yellowthroat, Common
3c-11a+	Warbler, Hooded
9b-4c	" , Wilson's
4-5; 8-10+	" , Canada
4b-10d+	Chat, Yellow-breasted
3d-10d+	Tanager, Summer
4-5; 9-11+	" , Scarlet
9b-4d	" , Western
SE	*Spindalis, Western*
SE	Tanager, Blue-gray
res.	Towhee, Eastern
res.	Sparrow, Bachman's
9b-5b+	" , Chipping
9b-5a	" , Clay-colored

Status		Species
res.		Sparrow,Field
10b-4c+		" , Vesper
7d-4d		" , Lark
9c-5c		" , Savannah
9d-4d		" , Grasshopper
10b-4b+		" , Henslow's
10c-2d		" , Le Conte's
9c-5c	*	" , Nelson's Sharp-tailed
9c-5c		" , *Saltmarsh Sharp-tailed*
res.	*	" , Seaside
11a-3c		" , Fox
10b-4d		" , Song
10b-4d		" , Lincoln's
10a-5c		" , Swamp
10a-5c+		" , White-throated
10a-5a+		" , White-crowned
10d-4b+		Junco, Dark-eyed
??		Longspur
NE		Bunting, Snow
res.		Cardinal, Northern
4-5; 9-10+		Grosbeak, Rose-breasted
10c		" , Black-headed
4a-11a+		" , Blue
3d-11c+		Bunting, Indigo
3d-11a+		" , Painted
9d-4d+		Dickcissel
4-6; 8-10+		Bobolink
res.		Blackbird, Red-winged
res.		Meadowlark,Eastern
10-1		" , Western
3-4; 9-10		Blackbird, Yellow-headed
10b-3c+		" , Rusty
10c-3d		" , Brewer's
res.		Grackle, Boat-tailed
res.		" , Common
4c-9c+		*Cowbird, Shiny*
res.		" , Brown-headed
3c-9b+		Oriole, Orchard
SE		" , Spot-breasted
8d-5a+		" , Baltimore
9b-4c+		" , *Bullock's*
11b-4b+		Finch, Purple
res.		" , House
11a-5c+		Siskin, Pine
10c-5d+		Goldfinch, American
12b-5a		Grosbeak, Evening
res.		Sparrow, House
Miami		" , Java

American Birding Association
Code of Ethics

Everyone who enjoys birds and birding must always respect wildlife, its environment, and the rights of others. In any conflict of interest between birds and birders, the welfare of the birds and their environment comes first.

1 Promote the welfare of birds and their environment.

- Support the protection of important bird habitat.
- Avoid stressing birds or exposing them to danger.
- Limit methods of attracting birds.
- Remain well back from nests, roosts, display areas, and feeding sites.
- Keep habitat disturbance to a minimum.

2 Respect the law and the rights of others.

3 Ensure that feeders, nest structures, and other artificial bird environments are safe.

- Maintain and clean feeders and nest structures regularly.
- Keep birds safe from predation from cats and other domestic animals.

4 Group birding, whether organized or impromptu, requires special care.

- Respect fellow birders. Share your knowledge, especially with beginners.
- Document unethical birding behavior, intervene if prudent, and notify appropriate individuals or organizations.
- Leaders should teach ethics through word and example,
- Limit group impact on birds and their environment, and others using the same area.

Please follow this code—distribute & teach it to others.

Index to Bird Species